Norma D. Logan

Power and Authority in the Victorian City

Comparative Studies in Social and Economic History 1

General editor: *J. R. Kellett*

*This book
is affectionately dedicated
to the members of B.A.A.*

Power and Authority in the Victorian City

DEREK FRASER

BASIL BLACKWELL · OXFORD

© Derek Fraser 1979

First published 1979 by
Basil Blackwell, Publisher
5 Alfred Street
Oxford OX1 4HB

All rights reserved. No part of this publication may be reproduced, stored in a retrieval system, or transmitted, by any form or by any means, electronic, mechanical, recording or otherwise, without the prior permission of Basil Blackwell Publisher.

British Library Cataloguing in Publication Data
Fraser, Derek
   Power and authority in the Victorian city.
   1. Municipal government — England — History — 19th century
   I. Title
   352′.008′0942   JS3078

ISBN   0-631-10561-1 (hardback)
ISBN   0-631-10571-9 (paperback)

Typeset by Malvern Typesetting Services Ltd
Printed in Great Britain by
Billing and Sons Ltd,
London, Guildford and Worcester

General Preface

Comparative Studies in Social and Economic History is a new series committed to the systematic examination of major historical themes in differing settings of time and place. All too frequently there has seemed to be no middle way between the learned monograph dealing with an historical episode in one narrow context and the more ambitious study generalizing at random from a bewilderingly wide-ranging background. Yet certain clear insights can be gained by a more controlled group of parallel and comparative studies. It is possible by means of concise individual *case studies* to underline those elements which are unique and particular to each topic's manifestation in a given time and place.

Each author in the present series will provide a framework for analysing a particular historical episode or problem in changing settings, and will also suggest a personal perspective in the opening and closing chapters.

Future comparisons in preparation will consider the ideals and practice of *Urban Planning* in four different contexts, and the experience of *Industrial Disputes* in Britain and America.

In the first inquiry Derek Fraser examines, through the study of a variety of nineteenth century cities, how and why municipal authorities became institutions with broad social purposes.

J. R. Kellett
Glasgow, April 1979

Contents

Acknowledgements ix

1 Municipal Reform 1
  Local Administration and the Coming of Reform 1
  Expectations of Reform 11
  A Municipal Revolution? 21

2 Liverpool 22
  The Impact of Municipal Reform 22
  The Council as Sanitary Reformer 36
  Reaction and the Resurgence of the Municipal Ideal 44

3 Leeds 51
  The Impact of Municipal Reform 51
  Sanitary Reform 58
  Reaction and Economy 68
  Municipal Revival 72

4 Birmingham 78
  Municipal Reform and Incorporation 78
  The Battle for Amalgamation 86
  False Starts — Reaction Before Achievement 95
  The Civic Gospel 101

5 Bristol, Leicester, Bradford and Sheffield *111*
   Bristol: The Evolution of Reform *112*
   Muckraking in Leicester *120*
   Bradford: Towards Municipal Socialism *130*
   Sheffield: A Difficult Passage to Reform *139*

6 Municipal Authority in Victorian Cities *149*
   The 1835 Revolution *149*
   The Municipalization of Local Government *151*
   The Establishment of Municipal Authority *157*
   The Creation and Accumulation of Powers *163*
   The Definition of a Positive Social Role *167*

   Notes *174*

   Bibliography *179*

   Index *185*

Acknowledgements

A work of synthesis must depend greatly upon the work of others and I am most grateful to the many scholars whose work I have consulted in the preparation of this book. I trust that in bringing academic research to a wider audience (one of the objects of the series), I have not distorted or misrepresented any of the valuable work that has been done in the field of nineteenth century urban history. Two people deserve my special thanks. My colleague Jack Reynolds has once more placed me in his debt by reading the book both at typescript and proof stage. Many of his valuable suggestions have been incorporated into the finished product. The general editor of the series, John Kellett, has been a model of diligence and concern. He spent a great deal of time correcting my grammar and smoothing the style. The book has been much improved by these and by his substantive suggestions. I am also much indebted to Mary Walker who typed the manuscript quickly and efficiently. Responsibility for errors and shortcomings remains mine alone.

Derek Fraser,
University of Bradford

One
Municipal Reform

LOCAL ADMINISTRATION AND THE COMING OF REFORM

English local government in the early nineteenth century was a remarkable patchwork whose infinite variety no contemporary could fully comprehend. The inconsistent mixture of historical, religious and administrative traditions which underlay the system was appropriate to a country that had been primarily governed locally rather than nationally for at least two centuries, a development that had encouraged local initiative and had proliferated regional variations. In the counties the Justices of the Peace reigned supreme, and the county bench possessed both administrative and judicial functions. The great German legal historian, Gneist, identified the unpaid justices, acknowledging the responsibilities of local administration as the great bulwark of English liberties. English Radicals, however, saw the county bench as the focus of a tyrannical oligarchy imposing class rule upon the people immune to its opinions. Despite the 'march of democracy' the appointed justices remained in control of county government until late-Victorian times and it was in the towns that reform of English local government began.

Nineteenth-century towns, in terms of their internal government, fell into two distinct groups, those incorporated and those unincorporated. Unincorporated towns had no charter, thus no corporation, and were under the aegis of the county bench and liable to pay the county rate. In some respects unincorporated towns did gradually gain a degree of independence of county rule and might be governed by a succession of boards; perhaps first by an improvement commission appointed under a local act early in the century, then by a local board of health under the 1848 Public Health

Act, then by a local government board under the 1858 Local Government Act, then by a sanitary authority under the 1872 Public Health Act and finally by an urban district council at the end of the century. The unincorporated towns, though gradually enjoying the benefits of an elected local authority, did not possess a corporation before 1835 or a town council after it. Many such towns did petition for a charter of incorporation and eventually gained corporate status, but those that did not remained outside the mainstream development of urban local government with which this book is concerned.

Urban local government in the corporate towns was the forcing house of municipal reform and it established the pattern of local administration which was eventually to be imposed upon the country as a whole. As elsewhere, there was great variety in the corporations that existed in the early nineteenth century, but there was one thing they all had in common, and which they shared with all other organs of local administration, and that was that they were ill fitted to meet the governmental needs of a rapidly growing and fast changing society. The corporations had been created in other times to meet problems different from those facing an emerging urban industrial society. Yet one seventh of the urban population of England lived under their rule in the 1830s, although many rapidly growing towns such as Manchester, Birmingham and Sheffield were without corporations. Whether a town was incorporated or not was not a function of size but a mere accident of history, whether a charter had been granted by the crown in past time. Those towns that had been favoured with a charter, which did include some of the growing industrial cities such as Liverpool, Leeds and Nottingham, were not necessarily thereby endowed with an effective form of local government. Corporations were private rather than public institutions, responsible to their members, the freemen, rather than to the citizens at large, and committed to corporate property interests rather than to the welfare of the town. Indeed the one compelling fact that demonstrated the ineffectiveness of corporations was that they had not been deemed suitable to exercise even minimal local government functions. As the 1835 Royal Commission report explained:

> It has been customary not to rely on the municipal corporations for exercising the powers incidental to good government. The powers granted by Local Acts of Parliament for various purposes have been from time to time conferred, not upon the municipal officers, but upon trustees or commissioners distinct from them, so that often the corporations have hardly any duties to perform. They have the nominal government of the town, but the efficient duties and the responsibility have been transferred to other hands.[1]

The corporations had become effete and so were in need of radical reform.

The actual pressure for reform, however, rested upon other facts than these and emerged directly out of the process of industrialization and urbanization itself. Despite their remoteness from their host communities, corporations in the eighteenth century were reasonably secure in their privileges, but the social dislocation contingent upon the industrial revolution exposed their limitations and generated a powerful demand for reform. Concern for effective town government was born of the population growth and mobility which characterized the industrial revolution and, in the early nineteenth century, reform of urban local government became a pressing necessity. There were four main planks in the reform case and they were all related to the wider social consequences of England's fundamental economic change during the reign of George III.

First, there was the growing problem of law and order in the towns, which was to be a compelling force for local government reform throughout the nineteenth century. The violent incidents, Luddism, Spa Fields, Pentridge and Peterloo, of the century's second decade were not perhaps typical of urban affairs, but they were very worrying to both national and local governors. Already a Prime Minister, Lord Liverpool, was bemoaning the fact that England was becoming ungovernable because of the volatility of these great cities with their undisciplined crowds. The lack of an effective civil police force was becoming a crucial factor in the attempt to create an ordered stable society, a fact recognized in Peel's exceptional measure in creating the Metropolitan Police force for the capital in 1829. Above all the Reform Bill riots of 1831, particularly in Bristol and Nottingham, which both had corporations, were convincing proof that municipal reform was necessary if only to maintain order.

The working-class crowds were one dimension of the new social structure of cities, the entrepreneurial middle class the other. The political and religious exclusiveness of the unreformed corporations became an increasingly irritating thorn in the side of the new commercial and industrial elite in the towns and hence the second aspect of the reform campaign. The traditional urban elite, mirrored in the composition of many corporations, had comprised gentlemen and merchants of the Tory-Anglican establishment. In the late eighteenth and early nineteenth centuries many new urban families who were dissenters in religion and Whig-Radical in politics established themselves through commerce and industry. Though rivalling the older elite in wealth they were usually excluded on religious and political grounds from membership of the corporations and so denied the offices of councilman, alderman, mayor and magistrate. Even the repeal of the Test and Corporation Acts in 1828, which allowed dissenters to become members of corporations, did not produce any great improvement from the nonconformist point of view. Though a small number of corporations, such as Nottingham, were dominated by Whig dissent, the vast majority were gratuitously proud of their pure Tory-Anglican composition. The Corporations were thus unable to reflect socially and politically the true balance of economic interests in the towns.

The third factor concerned the mode of appointment to corporations. Again this varied widely, and there was sometimes an element of popular participation where the designation of freemen was particularly broad. Despite the variety, the corporations were for the most part self-elected through co-option. No doubt as a means of ensuring that suitable leading citizens gained access to the corporation, the process of co-option (or other forms of self-election) had its advantages. By the early nineteenth century such advantages were outweighed by the corruption with which so many corporations were tainted, and so the Radicals identified the process of self-election as the source of the corporate evil and the means by which an illegitimate oligarchy maintained itself. When constructing a programme of reform to make England a more just society, the Radicals naturally placed considerable emphasis upon the denial of natural justice implicit in the self-elective constitution of the corporations.

Finally, and explaining the precise timing of municipal reform, there was the link between the 1832 Reform Act and the corporations. In order to bring the representative system more closely into line with a developing urban industrial society, the Whig ministry of Earl Grey had swept away many nomination boroughs and extended and unified the borough franchise. (Gash, 1953, 65-101). Since the freemen and other ancient rights voters were to retain the parliamentary vote for their lifetimes, and since the majority of corporate towns were still to return MPs, this left in the hands of the corporations considerable electoral power which, if past experience was followed, they were likely to use extensively and in a corrupt manner for the Tory interest in Parliamentary elections. In many places the only real evidence of corporate activity lay in the corrupt use of corporation influence and money at election time. The preservation of this electoral power would thus have frustrated the aims of the 1832 reform, and as *The Times* explained in 1833, 'the fact is that Parliamentary reform, if it were not to include Corporation reform likewise, would have been literally a dead letter.' That parliamentary and municipal reform were but two horses in the same harness was well illustrated by the remarks of one of their main supporters, Joseph Parkes, who in 1835 described municipal reform as 'our Postscript to the Reform Bills; in fact, Municipal Reform is the steam engine for the Mill built by Parliamentary Reform.'

It was therefore highly likely that the Whigs would introduce a municipal reform bill in the early 1830s, and indeed in 1833 Lord Althorp announced that he had such legislation ready to present. This was deferred pending a report by a Select Committee appointed in February 1833. After a few months this body decided that its task was far too extensive and in turn it recommended the appointment of a Royal Commission, which was created in July 1833. This was the second major Royal Commission set in train by the Whigs (the first had been that on the Poor Law established in February 1832). These two classic reports—the Poor Law Report of 1834 and the Municipal Corporations Report of 1835—firmly established the precedent of extensive enquiry before legislative action which was to be followed again and again throughout the century. No previous age knew as much of itself as did mid-nineteenth century England, with its mountain of blue books. The advantages of a Royal Commission over the previous popular select Committee were numerous. The membership of a Commission was not restricted to members of both houses of Parliament; it could call upon the active services of experts, rather than merely having them as witnesses; it could, of itself, perambulate the country seeking out evidence, rather than employ others to do so. Above all it had sufficient independence of Parliament to offer an authoritative and objective report. In so doing it fitted well with the novel utilitarian theories of Bentham, who advocated vigorous research and enquiry prior to legislation so that the full and impartial facts could be exposed. How could one know what would conduce to the greatest happiness of the greatest number unless all the relevant evidence had been studied and value free conclusions deduced? Here, if anywhere, lay the origin of scientific social legislation.

In theory the great reports of 1834 and 1835 were unbiased social research leading logically to objective policy recommendations: in practice both were propaganda for a preconceived course of legislative action. The Poor Law Commission was set up to condemn the Poor Law just as the Municipal Commission was set up to condemn the old corporations. Sir James Graham, who was a Whig minister when these two Royal Commissions were established, later advised Peel that 'a commission is most useful to pave the way for a measure which is preconcerted' and confirmed that in both the Poor Law and corporation cases 'the Government which granted the Enquiry contemplated and sought a specific change, and had the Commission as a pioneer for their measure.' Municipal historians should not therefore expect the report of the Royal Commission to be the fount of impartial knowledge as far as the unreformed corporations are concerned. Just how biased the report was is a matter of some debate. In the most famous history of English local government (Webb, 1908, 721) it was argued that 'the historical student must dismiss it as a bad case of a violent political pamphlet being, to serve Party ends, issued as a judicial report.' A more recent survey (Keith Lucas, 1952, 51) suggests that the report was 'on the whole an honest statement of the condition of the borough corporations . . . no exaggeration or misrepresentation was needed, for the bare statement of facts . . . was in itself enough to damn them completely.'

The bias inherent in the Royal Commission originated in its terms of reference and composition (Finlayson, 1963). It was instructed not simply to 'inquire into the existing state of the Municipal Corporations' but also to 'collect information respecting the defects in their constitution.' That there existed major defects was thus not at issue. Moreover, the persons appointed to the Commission were nearly all, as Lord Lyndhurst remarked, 'Whigs and something more.' Only two out of twenty were not Whig or Radical in politics; many were Benthamites. Lord Brougham had selected young and talented barristers who shared the Whigs' belief that a more representative form of local government was a pressing necessity. At the head of the Commission was John Blackburne, Radical MP for Huddersfield, who was an energetic chairman, anxious to present a report quickly, and who over-ruled cautious and dilatory commissioners. Above all, the secretary to the Commission, Joseph Parkes, ensured that the Whigs would get the kind of report they wanted. Parkes was a Radical lawyer who had a long-standing antipathy to corporations and who had acted as a liason between the Birmingham Political Union and the Whig ministry during the Reform Bill crisis. Though never in Parliament, he was connected to many who were, and was *persona grata* in both Whig and Radical camps. As Whig party agent he knew the advantages Tories derived from the corporations and their corrupt freemen voters. He made it clear that he would use the Commission to further political ends and he predicted to Francis Place

> I shall do great good in the Corporations Commission. I thoroughly . . . understand the Municipal question — what our civic institutions are and what they should be. We shall do our duty. . . . I augur no great political progress in this country till we obtain a popular elective municipal system.

With such a membership and so politically directed a leadership, it was predictable that the Commission's ultimate report would be a party document, for as Wellington commented,

> of course these individuals acted as Party men . . . this Inquiry has been instituted, these Gentlemen have been selected to conduct it . . . it is quite obvious that gossip and scandal were the object . . .[2]

Though the Commissioners might be accused of some preconceptions, they could certainly not be indicted for indolence. They worked quickly, industriously and efficiently. Parkes organized the work, dividing the country into circuits which the Commissioners would visit in pairs. He issued standardized questionnaires and arranged the drafting of local reports so that they could all be collated in a uniform manner. During the winter of 1834-5 Parkes and Blackburne began drafting a general report even though all the evidence was not yet complete. Though two Commissioners protested about the undue haste and ultimately refused to sign the report because the evidence was incomplete, Parkes was able to carry the Commission with him and the General Report was in ministers' hands in March 1835 and published the next month. The Commissioners had visited nearly three hundred places and had concluded that 246 corporations existed. Detailed local reports on 183 of these were printed as appendices to the General Report.

The Commissioners' general conclusions reflected both their predilections and the local evidence they had received. Parkes's Liberal connections ensured that wherever Commissioners went the local 'Liberal Caste' appeared in force at public enquiries. In general Liberal accusations were accepted at face value and incorporated into local reports, while Tory defences were summarily dismissed. Corporate maladministration was prominently displayed, good government minimized and judicial shortcomings exaggerated. The General Report was a massive indictment of the corporations' inefficiency, corruption and injustice, and its recommendation was strident:

> there prevails amongst the inhabitants of a great majority of the incorporated towns a general, and in our opinion, a just dissatisfaction with their Municipal Institutions . . . We therefore feel it to be our duty to represent to Your Majesty that the existing Municipal Corporations of England and Wales neither possess nor deserve the confidence of respect of Your Majesty's subjects, and that a thorough reform must be effected, before they can become, what we humbly submit to Your Majesty they ought to be, useful and efficient instruments of local government.[3]

There could be no more compelling justification for immediate municipal reform.

Armed with so powerful a case the Whigs quickly introduced a bill which was drafted by one of the Commissioners, J. R. Drinkwater, with frequent comments from Parkes. The bill proposed to sweep away the old corporations and replace them by elected councils with household suffrage and a three-year residence and ratepaying franchise. Freemen and aldermen were to be abolished; borough magistrates were to be elected by the council and one third of the council were to retire each year. Licensing was to be in the hands of the council, which would be headed by an elected mayor. Parkes, who had only with difficulty persuaded Melbourne, the Prime Minister, to accept household suffrage, was euphoric about the proposals:

> We clear the roost from top to bottom—Town Clerks and all—abolish all old names except Mayor and Town Clerk—give a simple Town Council—Magistrates elected by the Council, confirmed by Royal Commission, Council, $\frac{1}{3}$ to go out annually (not so good as bodily every 3 years) annual and public audits—all charities placed under the administration of a separate popular board—all licenses vested in Council—the only condemnable points magistrates for *life* and *3* years term of Rate paying.

However it is a smasher — a grand point to get Household suffrage, and a thorough purge of the existing Corporators . . . We *burke* the Freemen and by a clause which will be subject of great conflict close the doors for ever against all inchoate rights and future perpetuation of the freedom for the Parliamentary franchise.[4]

Rather unexpectedly, this surprisingly radical measure passed through the Commons with ease and at the end of July 1835 the bill went up to the Lords. The speed of passage in the lower house was wholly due to Peel's moderation. Demonstrating clearly the nature of Conservatism as opposed to reactionary Toryism, Peel admitted the need for reform, accepted the bill and contented himself with minor amendments of detail. He had in fact given due warning of this likely course of action by his reference in the Tamworth Manifesto to 'the reform of proved abuses' and by his refusal to wind up the Royal Commission during his short 1834–5 ministry. Tory peers, led by Lord Lyndhurst, were not so accommodating, and decided to oppose the bill root and branch. Peelite Conservatism buttered no parsnips with Lyndhurst, who exclaimed, when warned to follow Peel's line, 'Peel! What is Peel to me? Damn Peel!' The Municipal Corporations Bill promised both a major split in the Tory party and a major constitutional confrontation between Lords and Commons.

In the event neither developed, for the statesmanlike Peel refused to support any of the Lords' amendments that he could not in honour have supported in the Commons, and the Whig ministers jettisoned some of their more controversial proposals, agreeing to some compromises. One quarter of the council was to be made up of aldermen, elected by the council and to serve six years. This was to be of long-term significance, for the aldermen survived until 1974, and only then did England adopt the mayor-councillor limitation proposed by the Whigs in 1835. Councillors were to have a substantial property qualification, and in boroughs of over 6,000 population the town was to be divided into wards, which would take account of rateable value as well as mere numbers. Magistrates were to be appointed by the Crown (though Russell said he would sympathetically consider council nominations for the bench) and were to retain their licensing authority. The freemen, the most controversial element in the reform package, were in fact reprieved, and they retained their Parliamentary, though not their municipal, franchise. As amended, the bill received the royal assent in September 1835, and under the terms of the Municipal Corporations Act, 178 corporations were abolished and 178 town councils created in their stead. The municipal franchise was to be unified: all occupiers who had resided and paid rates in the borough for three years would vote for the whole council at the first election and thereafter annually for one third of the council. Mayor and aldermen would be elected by the councillors themselves and all debates were to be open and accounts publicly audited. Free, open, representative town government replaced self-elective, close oligarchy in the corporate towns. The Act also laid down a procedure for an unincorporated town to petition the Crown for a Charter of incorporation which would apply the benefits of the 1835 Act to a borough so endowed. It was, in short, a municipal revolution, and though Radicals like Place might bluster about the damaging compromises, Parkes, as much as anyone the moving spirit behind municipal reform, could put on a brave face, subdue his own misgivings and pronounce,

> *Politically* except for the discount of little *wards* the Bill is as good as ever it was. *Municipally* it is injured in the Crown Appointment of Justices. . . . Still the bill as a whole is more than we had any right to obtain this year—a full and more than an equivalent I think for the discount; and better such a bird in the hand than a better in the bush. . . . It is a practical victory over the Lords and Tory aristocracy . . . *I am content*.[5]

EXPECTATIONS OF REFORM

When Parkes had said that the municipal question was a matter of 'what our civic institutions are and what they should be,' he was not asserting that municipal reform would be judged only in its administrative context. It has been well argued that municipal reform must be related to its essentially political context if its significance is to be fully understood

(Finlayson, 1966). Both the fears and aspirations generated by municipal reform were closely related to political perspectives, and attitudes to the 1835 'revolution' were conditioned by political partisanship. The response to 1835 may conveniently be studied in terms of Whig, Tory and Radical assessment of municipal reform.

Whig ministerial concerns were centred upon the reform of judicial administration and the distinct possibility of party advantage (or at the very least the removal of the enemy's advantages). There is little doubt that, however reforming Whig ministries might be, they would tolerate no threats to order. It was the same government that condemned to death 'Swing' rioters of 1830 and introduced the Reform Bill; the same administration that transported the Tolpuddle martyrs and sustained municipal reform. Both in town and county there was an urgent need for police reform since the traditional law enforcement agencies were inadequate to meet the challenge of an augmented and restless population. The Reform Bill riots of 1831 have already been mentioned; they had convinced the Whigs that even in corporate towns the maintenance of civil order was impossible in times of popular excitement. The Reform Bill crisis had also provided the spectre of a citizen militia, which no member of Grey's cabinet, no matter how radical, could contemplate without the most profound alarm. When Attwood placed the Birmingham Political Union upon a semi-military footing in order to maintain public order, the possibility of an independent popular vigilante force outside the control of the normal channels of authority was a far greater threat to the sovereignty of property than was any amount of rick burning or crowd violence. The government was duly warned that it must itself reassert order in the urban chaos or it would have to yield up its powers to bodies alien to the legal constitution. The County Police Act of 1839 attempted to introduce effective policies into the rural areas and municipal reform was geared to the same task for the boroughs. Indeed the only compulsory duty imposed upon the new town councils was the formulation of a watch committee and the establishment of a borough police force.

Concern for the maintenance of urban order was allied to a less elevated Whig expectation of party advantage. Parkes, a master of election intrigue and manipulation, was on hand to put the party gain in electoral perspective. The Corporations Bill, he promised, 'will be poison to Toryism,' and he estimated that 'with such a degree of Municipal Reform we may defy Peel and any union of Tories or Coalitions he may effect.' The reasoning was simple. Most of the corrupt unreformed corporations were Tory and so their abolition would remove much Tory influence at election time. The new councils were confidently expected to be predominantly Liberal and would therefore yield electoral advantage to the Whigs. There was thus some point to Lyndhurst's accusation that

> this Bill was not a Bill for the Reform of Corporations but a Bill brought in to consolidate and strengthen the party by whom it was brought in . . . it was a party job intended to . . . destroy the Conservative party in the country, in order that their opponents might . . . recover their political influence.[6]

It was not so much a removal of electoral corruption as its transfer from one side to the other of the political stage, for as *The Times* exclaimed, 'it is nothing more nor less than one enormous Whig-Radical job . . . to strengthen and consolidate still further the political party by which the commission has been issued and the measure framed.'

It was particularly in the attempted suppression of the freemen that the party bias was so pronounced, for in towns such as Liverpool where they were numerous, the notoriously venal freemen were overwhelmingly Tory. Their disfranchisement would indeed be an amendment to the 1832 Reform Act by a 'side-wind,' for in that act voting rights of freemen had been preserved. This was the aspect of municipal reform which angered the otherwise moderate Peel, and he wrote spiritedly:

> After reviewing the returns, they find the freemen vote in the Conservative interest . . . forthwith it is proposed to abolish freemen . . . the Corporation Bill . . . rejects with scorn the doctrine that poor men are not fit to exercise political power—when that

doctrine aids democratic influence—but this same Bill disfranchises other poor men who have been guilty of the crime of supporting Conservative principles. It assumes that the Irish pauper who has resided three years in Manchester and Liverpool and can get an active democrat to pay up for him his shilling rate, is well qualified for electoral trust; but the man who has served an apprenticeship of seven years; the Englishman by birth; the native of the town; . . . he is to be dispossessed . . . can anyone doubt the animus, the bounty on Radicalism, the punishment of Conservative principle in humble life?[7]

Peel could not support Lyndhurst's wilder demands, but he might well have echoed the noble Lord's conclusion that 'it was a Whig measure—Whig in its principle, Whig in its character and Whig in its object.'

Naked partisanship perhaps masked a subtle form of political motivation. One of the objects of the 1832 Reform Act had been to create an alliance between the Liberal middle class and the Whig landed gentlemen. To cement this alliance, bourgeois votes had been created and bourgeois spheres of influence designated in the new urban constituencies. The Act of 1835, which formalized the legal context in which the urban elite might establish hegemony over its community, was a further stage in the same process. Moreover, municipal reform generated a spoils system upon which deprived middle-class leaders might feast, and Parkes was all too well aware 'that the Liberals are naturally looking to the municipal patronage—County Attorneys to Town Clerkships—Liberal Bankers to Treasurerships etc. etc.' The events of the years 1832 and 1835 were thus stages in the Whig search for a role for the bourgeoisie in the political system, a search which had begun in the 1820s, when Earl Grey had drawn attention to the great strides the middle classes had made in the accumulation of wealth. Municipal reform sealed a compact between urban and landed elite.

Tory propaganda found much to bluster about in the Whig political bias of the whole exercise and much Tory outpouring was conditioned by this. Beyond party issues lay a Tory concern to defend the rights of property and to warn of the dangerous consequences of municipal reform. Tory leaders saw attacks upon property throughout the Corporations Bill, in the disposition of corporate property and charity funds, in the robbery of freemen and town clerks alike, and in the attack upon corporations as institutions. Their amendments were correspondingly geared to defend the rights of property (to preserve the rights of freemen as a form of property, to secure compensation for town clerks) and to preserve propertied leadership in the new system (by life aldermen, crown appointment of magistrates, wards in smaller boroughs and a property qualification for councillors). In Tory strategy the nominative principle was more likely than the elective to produce respectable government by the wealthy.

And it was fear of what the democratic municipal franchise might throw up that underlay all Tory protests. Some feared that the Reform Act itself made a republic likely, and 1835 simply confirmed the tendency. One Tory peer told Peel that councillors would be 'men of the most revolutionary violence and least character in the boroughs' and that church and monarchy could not be defended without loyal corporations. Similarly, Lyndhurst viewed corporations as a barrier between the throne and raw democracy, and warned the House of Lords that if the corporations fell, then 'the Church would come next and the hereditary peerage of the realm afterwards.' Tory fears were well illustrated in the petitions against municipal reform presented by the Leeds Corporation. When the bill was first introduced the Corporation denounced it as 'a sweeping measure . . . calculated to throw municipal government into the hands of Political Partizans and religious sectaries opposed to the best and most sacred Institutions of the country.' The Lords' opposition to the bill was strongly supported, and the upper house was reminded that the effect would be to give power to 'a class of persons who though numerically the greatest are from their education, habits and station in life not likely to be the most intelligent or independent.' If a bill was to pass it must 'secure to property that fair and legitimate influence which it ought to possess . . . in giving efficiency to the powers and functions of the Governing Body.'[8]

In the event the municipal franchise did not turn out as

democratic as had been feared, for the residence and ratepaying qualifications reduced the number of voters often below that of the parliamentary register which was based upon the £10 suffrage as against household suffrage of municipal elections (Keith-Lucas 1952, 59–63). Nevertheless, Radicals hoped and Tories feared that municipal reform would create local democracy, and the fears of the latter rested firmly on the hopes of the former. Radical attitudes may be divided between political and 'Philosophic' Radicalism. Political Radicals saw municipal reform as one battle in the war against a ramified aristocratic establishment whose hold on British institutions had to be broken. Clearly the Whigs were part of this establishment, and the political chameleon, Parkes, who ran with Whig hares but hunted with the Radical hounds, was prepared to use Whiggery to achieve a higher Radical purpose. To Francis Place he wrote:

> Far from perfect as the Corporation Act was—and reduced as was its original degree of perfection—yet it has done or rather will in its effects *do the business*, & that at no distant time. The Unincorporated towns will lust after & soon accomplish the destruction of their Self Elect, and the Country magisterial & fiscal Self Elect will next and early be mowed down by the scythe of Reform. The *Franchise* . . . must lead to a uniformity and extension of the Parliamentary franchise. The new town councils are of course compounded of much local *Whiggism* a deleterious ingredient. This is unavoidable because Unions could alone have defeated the Common Enemy. But the Rads will in a year or two work all that scum off. 3 years are only a moment in the life of a nation. . . . The Tories are burked, no resurrection for them. The Whigs . . . are an unnatural party standing between the People and the Tory aristocracy—chiefly for the pecuniary value of the offices and the vanity of power. Their hearse is ordered . . .[9]

Parkes set the tone for both metropolitan and provincial Radicals, and when, as he predicted, the unincorporated towns sought to destroy 'their Self Elect' it was with an overtly political object that incorporation petitions were launched. In Birmingham Thomas Attwood looked to reformed corporations to take over the political work hitherto performed by the political unions. In 1837 he told a town meeting that:

One of the main objects of the bill, for giving corporations to the new boroughs . . . was to establish real and legal Political Unions in every borough which would supersede the necessity of such formidable bodies as he, Mr. Attwood, had the honour of being head of . . . they should thus possess for the future acknowledged legal organs which would enable them to exercise in a strictly legal and safe way all the political functions which he had been endeavouring to work out through all the dangers and difficulties which had always surrounded the Political Union . . . it would give the people a better and more efficient means of making their knowledge known and their power felt.[10]

The political unions had begun, and the town councils would complete, the war against the aristocracy, and the most unequivocal statement of the essentially political nature of municipal reform was provided by Richard Cobden. It was he who roused Manchester from its manorial slumber with his great pamphlet *Incorporate Your Borough*, and he did so with a stirring battle cry against the landed aristocracy:

The battle of our day is still against the aristocracy . . . The lords of Clumber, Belvoir, and Woburn, although they can no longer storm your town, and ransack your stores and shops, at the head of their mailed vassals, are as effectually plundering your manufacturers and their artizans; . . . And must you tamely submit to this pillage, or, like your ancestors of old, will you not resist the aristocratic plunderers? If the latter then imitate your forefathers by union and co-operation. . . . [and make] Manchester . . . the leader in the battle against monopoly and privilege. In a word Incorporate Your Borough . . . and thus place for ever the population of our town and neighbourhood beyond the control of a booby squirearchy.[11]

Victorian town halls were thus to be fortresses in the struggle against the country estates and their control over national government and institutions.

'Philosophic' Radicals certainly shared these political aspirations and hoped that municipal reform would bring nearer that democratic form of government which in their mentor's teaching would create the greatest happiness to the greatest number. 'Philosophic' Radicals were a loose intellectual group who had some connection with the great philosopher Jeremy Bentham. Partly because they were a very varied and individualist company, and partly because Bentham's prolific output was digested in differing degrees by members of the group, there was no one Benthamite school of thought on any one question. Bentham had laid out a system of government for what has been termed his 'Ideal Republic' in his great *Constitutional Code*, but this was not published until 1843, some years after his death, and it might itself have led to some inconsistency of view (Peardon, 1951). Both contemporaries and historians were much confused over just what the adjective 'Benthamite' meant, and an academic debate has developed over the role of Bentham, Benthamites and Benthamite ideas in the growth of state intervention in the nineteenth century. The Benthamite connection with municipal reform is equally obscure. The Webbs described the 1835 Act as containing 'the pure milk of Benthamism,' whereas a recent researcher maintained that a Benthamite blueprint would have led to a form of municipal socialism and that compared to real Benthamism the 1835 Act was small beer indeed. Moreover, while Bentham's preference for all powerful single local authorities was clear, it was under the original direction of Chadwick, an avowed Benthamite, that a fragmented and overlapping system of authorities was created — Poor Law Union, Local Boards of Health, Sanitary Authorities, School Boards etc. As Redlich and Hirst noticed, Bentham

> teaches the desirability of concentrating the whole administration of a district in the hands of a single executive organ, although . . . his love of differentiation led some of his practical, but unintelligent, followers to multiply local authorities.[12]

Keeping these qualifications in mind, it remains true that some Benthamite or 'Philosophic' Radicals could see in municipal reform the seeds of a wider local government system with more than simple political objectives. Perhaps in this they were carrying out Bentham's teaching; perhaps they had their own preconceived notions which Benthamite thinking rationalized. It has been well remarked that many of the Benthamites were already of mature years before they met the great man, and his mind may simply have given logical coherence to their existing ideas (Roberts, 1959). Two in particular, Francis Place and J. A. Roebuck, glimpsed a municipal future which might indeed lead to a form of local socialism. They collaborated in a series of pamphlets entitled *Pamphlets for the People* which publicized their vision of the true potential of municipal reform. They also launched a short-lived newspaper, the *Municipal Corporation Reformer*.

Roebuck, Radical MP for Bath, laid great stress upon the educational potential of municipal reform. Indeed, as soon as the first municipal elections had been held, he advised that 'the Town Councils ought immediately to open schools for the poor and have them taught upon an enlarged and liberal plan,' a policy implemented in Liverpool. Roebuck conceived of education in its widest sense, hence 'the pleasures, amusements and comforts of the inhabitants ought also, as greatly affecting their education, to come under the cognizance and superintendence of the Council.' The town hall, he said, should be a 'People's Hall' where lectures and meetings could be held, and 'it might thus be rendered an extremely efficient instrument in the improvement of the manners and habits of the People.'[13] Like others, Roebuck was disappointed that the 1835 Act had not gone further in designating a useful administrative role for the reformed corporations. When the bill was still under discussion, he himself sketched out the municipal image on a broad canvass:

> Powers for the due lighting of the towns and supplying the inhabitants with water should be entrusted to the corporations. . . . In the same way all the public charities—and, advancing one step further—all institutions of education supported by the people, should be in a great degree, under their immediate and direct control. All public markets also, all matters of police come necessarily under the same management. In short everything affecting the well being of the neighbourhood . . . ought to be considered as the business, and coming within the field, of corporate administration.[14]

Francis Place was a veteran London Radical who had masterminded the metropolitan parliamentary reform movement and he understandably agreed with the political strategy of Cobden and Attwood, viewing councils as democratic invaders into aristocratic territory. To this he allied a positive municipal administrative role which was largely absent from their concept of municipal reform. It was Place who provided the most lucid exposition of the potential of municipal reform in a comprehensive ground plan of local government. He drafted a synopsis of the principles, organization and administration of local government, which, he argued, ought to be the basis of the corporation reform legislation. His plan appeared in the prospectus for the Radicals' impending publication the *Municipal Corporation Reformer*, 60,000 copies of which were distributed. Place's ideas are worth citing at length because his scheme was the most comprehensive analysis of the potential administrative role of the new town councils that appeared during the 1830s.

He began, like Roebuck, with the general proposition that municipal government was created by the people 'to promote their common welfare,' from which it followed that 'town governments should exist only for the mutual advantage of the people.' Place focused attention on the local deliberative assembly, which should be elected by universal ratepayer suffrage with the ballot and without any property qualification for members. In describing this assembly's functions, Place indicated the broad horizons he conceived for municipal government:

1. Administration of public property held for general purposes, so as to obtain the greatest possible amount of revenue, and thus enable it to reduce the local taxation to a minimum.
2. Surveillance and payment of the magistrates, officers of the courts, all other officers and servants, the police, etc. etc., maintenance and suprintendence of the gaol or gaols.
3. Paving, lighting, cleansing, maintenance and improvement of the thoroughfares, and where possible, the supply of water.
4. Maintenance of public buildings and works, such as the town hall, the market places, bridges, harbours, docks, water courses, sewers etc.
5. Administration of trusts for hospitals, schools, and charities.
6. Making of bye laws for its own regulation, assessment of local taxes, appointment and dismissal of clerks and servants.[15]

It was a broad vision and, as Place and Roebuck knew well, it was one whose realization was threatened by the limitations of the 1835 legislation.

A MUNICIPAL REVOLUTION?

In summary, then, the 1835 municipal revolution was perceived with varying perspectives. The political spectrum threw up a range of interpretations of municipal reform — an agency for improved law and order, a Whig political engine for the middle class, an attack upon property and the harbinger of revolutionary change, a weapon in the political assault upon aristocratic power, a vehicle for the promotion of the community's welfare. A variegated conception of the effects of 1835 was imposed upon a local government system, which was itself infinitely varied. The outcome was thus difficult to predict. Yet in this confusion one thing was certain: that traditions of local sovereignty and antipathy to centralization would ensure that the pace and direction of urban government would be determined by local initiative and practice and not by general legislation. And so the student of the nineteenth century municipal question, in Parkes's phrase, of 'what our civic institutions are and what they should be,' must examine local and not central policy. To understand the way town government developed in Victorian England we must explore municipal reform on the ground, in the towns themselves. Hence the rest of this book is devoted to an analysis of urban local government as it progressed in individual communities. Three cities — Liverpool, Leeds and Birmingham — are examined in some depth, and a further four — Bristol, Leicester, Bradford and Sheffield — are more summarily reviewed. By comparing developments in these seven cities, which represent a fair sample of urban society, we may hope to chart and understand the establishment of municipal authority in Victorian England.

Two
Liverpool

THE IMPACT OF MUNICIPAL REFORM

The Corporation of Liverpool was an old established institution originating in a charter granted by King John in 1207. Under its aegis Liverpool had grown into the leading provincial port of England and, with dockland development, the Corporation had gained in property and wealth. Though nominally responsible to the town's freemen (who voted in mayoral and Parliamentary elections) the Corporation was a self-elective oligarchy of Tory-Anglican mercantile interests. One of the great evils of affairs in Liverpool in the early nineteenth century was the political role of the notoriously venal freemen; and Liberal and Dissenting groups (the political opposition to the Corporation) repeatedly tried to disfranchise the freemen as part of an attack upon the entrenched Tory Anglican oligarchy. The opening up of the Corporation was the ultimate aim, but this could not be achieved by local action, and it required the external assault of the municipal Corporations Commission to break the corporate monopoly.

In fact Liverpool Corporation came out of the municipal enquiry quite well, for although undoubtedly a 'close corporation' it was not indicted for corruption or maladministration. The Commission reported that

> in the main, the Corporation have evinced economy and good management in their affairs; that as magistrates they are attentive to their duties, and careful of the due regulation of the Borough; and that, as its governing body their conduct seems to have been materially influenced by a desire to promote its welfare.[1]

Historians have treated Liverpool Corporation less sympathetically. An eminent local scholar (Muir, 1907, 309) writing early in the present century commented that the Corporation did not regard itself as in any sense charged with the general welfare of the community, while more recently an American historian (Vigier, 1907, 179–83) has issued a general condemnation of the Corporation's failure to meet the challenge of urbanization and industrialization. These views are conditioned somewhat by an appreciation of what municipal government eventually became. The Corporation of Liverpool is thus judged by a yardstick of a later date rather than by the standards of its own time.

Yet to contemporaries the great evil of the Corporation was not its lack of a comprehensive social policy but its rigid exclusiveness, perpetuated by its system of self-election based on co-option. Liverpool's leading reform journalist explained the position:

> The simple facts are that members of the Common Council elect each other—that they consist of a round of sons, brothers and cousins—that they are an exclusive body both in religion and politics—that no merchant, however eminent, no Dissenter, however distinguished for his talents character and services has the most remote chance of obtaining a place in that privileged body.[2]

Municipal reform was the remedy and the 1835 act made possible popular participation in local government. Inevitably the first municipal elections of December 1835 were trials of strength between the former holders of and the contenders for municipal power. Though Tories might profess to exclude politics from municipal affairs, it was recognized that the elections would be 'more fierce and acrimonious than the contests we have hitherto witnessed at our general elections . . . the elections will be so many petty civil wars.'[3]

· In this Liverpool civil war the Liberal challengers were overwhelming victors, winning the first elections by 43 seats to 5. The composition of the new Council when aldermen had been elected by the councillors was 58–6 in favour of the Liberals. It was a dramatic assumption of power by Whigs and Dissenters who had previously been excluded from

Corporation affairs. Powerless in the Council chamber, the defeated Tories fell back on propaganda, using such ephemeral publications as the *Liverpool Satirist* to mock the new elite. The new political masters made their power manifest by purging the administration and rewarding their own party faithful. They also set about retrieving the £105,000 borough fund that had been alienated by the old Corporation in order to pay the salaries of Anglican clergymen. This was a common ploy by which traditional local governors were able to deprive their successors of the accumulated corporate funds. Though Tories (as in Leeds) might claim that this was a charitable act, Liberals saw it as an insult to the burgesses and as a deliberate blow aimed at the political authority of the reformed Council. The return of the alienated borough fund became a symbolic battle between old and new forces of local government. A two-year legal wrangle ended in a compromise out-of-court settlement in 1838, which included the repayment of the disputed £105,000.

Reformers were well satisfied with the outcome of the legal dispute, and they were equally content with what they deemed the benevolent effects of municipal reform. One of the most active of the new councillors was the radical Joshua Walmsley, the first chairman of the watch committee. He made an important speech in October 1836 reviewing the new Council's progress. The speech was published as a pamphlet entitled *What Have The Council Done?* and may be taken to represent contemporary views about the aspirations and achievement of municipal reform. Walmsley emphasized the great burden that councillors bore in committee work and judged that 'they have laboured day and night to deserve that honour and confidence which the people conferred upon them.' He identified the reform of the borough police force as the primary task of the new Council. A new force of 360 men was established under Walmsley's guidance with Michael J. Witty as head constable. Walmsley claimed that the new force had cut the crime rate, and that Witty's sensible management had established Liverpool's police force as the best provincial constabulary (Cockcroft, 1974). The new regime had reformed local justice by making courts more efficient and accessible and by the appointment of a stipendiary magistrate. The Council had also effected important financial reforms which had resulted in savings of over £10,000. Above all, the Council was subject to the popular will through the annual elections. Walmsley believed that 'the influence of popular opinion' was the ultimate guarantor of municipal efficiency.

Efficient administration, especially in police and judicial affairs, economy and popular election — these were the aims of municipal reform. There was, as yet, no great vision of a wider responsibility for municipal government. Yet one area of social policy was within the Council's authority, and Walmsley proudly recorded the new dimensions in the Corporation schools question. The Corporation schools, which dated from the 1820s, had previously been almost exclusively filled by Protestants. The new Council, by adopting the so-called 'Irish system' of readings from the Bible, had opened up the schools to Roman Catholic pupils as well. This attempt to provide non-denominational education was of more than just local significance and its historian has called it 'The Crucial Experiment' (Murphy, 1959).

The rise and fall of the Corporation schools experiment may be simply charted in an analysis of the religion of the pupils at the two schools. Prior to 1836 probably well over ninety per cent of pupils were Anglicans. Thereafter a change took place (see Table 2.1).

Table 2.1 Liverpool Corporation Schools 1838–42

	Total number of pupils	Percentage Roman Catholic
1838	1718	54
1840	1686	55
1842	1581	8

For a few years the schools were inter-denominational, and despite the opposition nearly half of the pupils were Protestants. Yet the schools question gave to the old Tory-Anglican interest a convenient political lever with which to pry the Liberals from municipal power. A Protestant backlash was led by a fiery Ulster minister, the Rev. Hugh M'Neile, who was able, with doubtful veracity, to assert that the Bible was excluded from Corporation schools. A strong anti-Catholic working-class prejudice was aroused which not only led to many Protestant withdrawals from the schools but also delivered many Council seats to the Tories. There were other issues, such as dock warehousing, which made the Council unpopular, but it was the religious aspect of the schools question which made municipal affairs in Liverpool so acrimonious in the early Victorian years. The relentless harrying of the Liberals whittled away their majority. By 1840 the Tories had more councillors than did the Liberals, whose power depended on their monopoly of the aldermanic seats. The 1841 election saw the Tories regain power, with the advantage of the aldermen now resting with them (see Table 2.2).

Table 2.2 *Political Composition of Liverpool Council 1835-42*

	Councillors		Aldermen		Whole council	
	Liberal	Tory	Liberal	Tory	Liberal	Tory
1835–6	43	5	15	1	58	6
1836–7	38	10	15	1	53	11
1837–8	34	14	15	1	49	15
1838–9	31	17	16	0	47	17
1839–40	30	18	16	0	46	18
1840–41	23	25	16	0	39	25
1841–42	15	33	7	9	22	42

THE IMPROVEMENT QUESTION

It was a remarkable reversal of political fortunes by which Liverpool 'returned to its old vomit of Toryism' and it set the seal on a Conservative control of Liverpool municipal Council which was to last for half a century. The new majority reverted to its exclusively Anglical educational policy and nearly all Roman Catholic children were withdrawn from the Corporation schools. The Liverpool Council was clearly not going to find its wider role in comprehensive education, but while

Conservatives pointedly reversed Liberal educational policy, they continued and developed Liberal public health policy. Here was the field which was to commit the Council to a more interventionist role in the coming years, and the crucial turning point lay in the 1840s.

The Liberal Council had obtained a new Improvement Act in 1837 and had amended local building regulations in 1839. In 1840 a health committee was first mooted, and on assuming power the Tories inherited plans for a 'Health of the Town' Act which was passed in 1842. Though the powers in this act were limited, the very passage of the legislation was significant, for, in the words of the Corporation's historian (White, 1951, 36), 'the Council . . . formally accepted some general responsibility for the health of the citizens.' That this responsibility would soon be broadened was the result of a growing local awareness of the hazards to public health endemic in the Liverpool environment. The man who did more than any other to publicize the sanitary evils of the town was Dr. William Henry Duncan, soon to be the country's first medical officer of health.

Duncan's propaganda found three outlets. First, he provided Edwin Chadwick with a 'Report on the Sanitary State of the Labouring Classes in the Town of Liverpool' which was both printed in the local reports appended to Chadwick's and cited by Chadwick in his own survey (Chadwick, 1842, 92). Chadwick's great report of 1842 was one of the outstanding Blue Books of the whole Victorian period and it stirred the public conscience. Liverpool was one of the first towns to act in the wake of the Chadwick Report. Duncan's second broadside took the form of two lectures delivered to the Liverpool Literary and Philosophical society in 1843. A pamphlet based upon the lectures was published by Joshua Walmsley under the title *The Physical Causes of the High Rate of Mortality in Liverpool*. The third barrage from the Duncan armoury was his evidence to the Royal Commission on the State of Large Towns which was printed in the appendix to the first report published in 1844. Another Liverpool man, the active Conservative Councillor Samuel Holme, a builder, was chairman of the Liverpool Tradesmen's Conservative

Association and was to be a prominent advocate of the extension of the town's water supply. He was a leading municipal figure for twenty years — Councillor in St. Peter's Ward from 1842 to 1845, in Rodney Street Ward from 1846 to 1849, in South Toteth Ward from 1850 to 1853; Alderman 1853–1864; and Mayor in 1852. He also presented evidence to the Royal Commission which systematically explored the possibilities of environmental control.

By the mid-1840s nobody could any longer believe that Liverpool was a healthy place, for Duncan had demonstrated that Liverpool had a higher mortality rate than any other large town, even including London. In 1845 the mayor called a meeting to launch a Liverpool branch of the Health of Towns Association, which further publicized the mounting evidence on Liverpool's dire need for sanitary regulation. Once the public was made aware of the public health issue itself, the question of what agency should be responsible for improvement was increasingly raised. Strangely enough, Liverpool was endowed not with too few improvement institutions but too many. In addition to the Council and the Select Vestry (the Poor Law organization), Liverpool also had Commissioners of Paving and Sewerage (usually known as the Highway Board) and two private water companies, while the out-townships had their own parochial institutions. This multiplicity of bodies with over-lapping jurisdictions emerged as the key problem in the social and political structure of Liverpool in the mid-1840s.

Lyon Playfair, in the second report of the Royal Commission on Large Towns and Populous Districts, drew attention to the powers in the Liverpool local acts and 'their want of consolidation and inconvenient distribution to distinct and sometimes opposing authorities'; while James Newlands, the borough engineer, reviewing the sanitary history of the town in 1858, commented on an 'anomalous and absurd' situation in which 'there were several governing bodies exercising powers and functions exceedingly inconsistent and therefore sanitary works could scarcely be called on at all.' Samuel Holme had made the same point in 1844:

These various boards consist of active men well versed in local affairs, but it has always appeared to me that unity of purpose is not obtained by having separate committees of action. I think that if these bodies could be amalgamated, and our watching, police, lighting, sewering and cleansing, together with the regulation of our buildings, were all placed under one committee acting in unison . . . there would be no jealousy of separate power and by the abolition of the cumbrous machinery of separate boards or rather its re-arrangement under one head, unity of purpose and vigour of action would be obtained.[4]

There was agreement on the need for consolidation of powers, but no exact consensus on which body should exercise those powers. There were three possibilities. First, the Select Vestry seemed appropriate, since so much disease was associated with destitution, and disease prevention measures were of significance for the Poor Law. Second, an enlarged version of the existing Highways Board, which would have involved membership partly directly elected by the ratepayers and partly nominated by the Council, was mooted. Third was the Council itself. That the main municipal institution was not overwhelmingly identified as the obvious public health agency was symptomatic of the uncertainty of contemporary opinion on the proper role of local government. Though without much conviction, local opinion accepted the notion that the Council should sponsor a bill through Parliament, the 1846 Liverpool Sanitary Act, which was a milestone in British social history.

The preamble to the Act explained the overwhelming need for amalgamation of powers throughout the whole borough. The aim of the Act was

> the Improvement of the Health and Comfort and the Diminution of the Disease and Mortality of the Inhabitants throughout the whole of the said Borough of Liverpool; and it is expedient that the Powers to be granted for the said Purpose should be combined under one management and should be uniform throughout the whole of the said Borough.[5]

The Act laid down the appointment of a Health Committee of the Council as the main executive agency and endowed the Corporation with wide powers of environmental control.

Clauses 113 and 114, for instance, authorized the Council to compel owners of houses to provide privies and to insist that all new houses would have to include proper sanitary arrangements. Perhaps most significant of all, the 1846 Act authorized the appointment of officers to enforce the powers — an inspector of nuisances, a borough engineer and, crucially, a medical officer of health. Though national legislation did not make the appointment of a M.O.H. mandatory until 1872, Liverpool, by means of a private local act, was the first place to take up the idea of a medical officer, first suggested in the Chadwick Report.

The appointment of Dr. W. H. Duncan as M.O.H. in January 1847 opened a new chapter in both Liverpool's sanitary and municipal history. Duncan could begin work on cleansing England's most insanitary town, with its special problem of immigrant Irish poor, and the Liverpool Corporation was designated as the borough's prime local government institution with wide powers over the local environment. The process of amalgamation of powers, hesitantly commenced in 1836, was now well advanced. Taking advantage of powers vested in the 1835 Municipal Corporations Act, the Liverpool Commission of Watch Lamps and Scavenging which dated from 1748 transferred its authority to the new Council in 1836. By the 1846 Act the Council adopted the powers of the Commission of Paving and Sewerage (usually called the Highways Board) which had first been appointed in 1830, together with powers which related to the suburban Toxteth Park under an act of 1842. It also took over the powers of commissioners to supply water for public purposes. The Council was now authorized to make sanitary regulations, to build sewers, to control street improvement and to cleanse and pave the highways. It was empowered to levy five rates (sewer, paving, general, lighting and fire) and could also levy an improvement rate for a specific purpose. Having accumulated new powers in 1846, the Liverpool Council went even further in the following year by embarking on the cardinal sanitary issue of water supply. This was to test the very will and authority of the Corporation itself.

Closely bound up with public awareness of Liverpool's

insanitary condition in the 1840s was a widespread dissatisfaction with existing water supplies. The two private water companies were criticized for inadequate and intermittent supply, and although much blame attached to landlords, nevertheless the whole water issue originated, as one of the protagonists explained, in 'a public attack upon the water companies . . . forgetting that those unfortunate companies had been struggling for years through great difficulties and that they were the only parties who had brought water at all.' The private enterprise system did have its defenders, and the director of one of the water companies reminded Liverpool of the wider achievements of

> the spirit of private enterprise which had called public works into action and rendered them by persevering industry, whether the result has proved losing or profitable to the capitalists engaged in them, sources of benefit and convenience to the community at large.[6]

Despite the apparent altruism of private enterprise, many became convinced that for a commodity so essential as water, public provision was necessary. Samuel Holme, who had publicized Liverpool's sanitary problems, was a leading propagandist in the campaign for a public water supply. In 1843 he read a paper to the Polytechnic Society in which he asserted that 'This town will never be supplied as it ought to be while we are dependent on private companies. The supply ought to be provided by the public authorities. . . . Paid for by a local rate levied on property, and freely distributed for the benefit of all.' In this paper, as in his evidence to the 1844 Royal Commission, he expressed gratitude to the private companies for providing water when public authorities had declined to do so. Yet the intolerable facts of life in Liverpool made mere gratitude for past efforts inadequate. As Holme argued,

> Water is as essential to the health and comfort of mankind as the air we breathe; and when mankind congregate in masses, counted only by tens of thousands, it is essential to the public health that it should be most abundant, not doled out to yield 30 per cent interest, but supplied from the public rates and at the net cost.[7]

Holme's decisive piece of propaganda was his important pamphlet *Want of Water* (1845) in which he clearly argued the collectivist case against private control of water supply:

> The public body is under public control. It is answerable to a constituency for its acts. It has no private interests to serve and all its deliberations are under the public eye. . . . A private company on the contrary has a pecuniary interest at stake . . . its deliberations are with closed doors . . . self interest is the ruling motive and the smallest supply at the highest rate produces the most satisfying dividends. I do not say that a public body ought therefore to become the butchers and bakers of a community but . . . water is as necessary to the health and welfare of the community as air . . . *public bodies must not be permitted to trade* . . . but in this case they will purchase [the private companies] for public benefit only and it will be as proper for them to do so as it is for them to tax us for our local government or to make our public sewers. The health of the town demands it.[8]

There was no effective reply to Holme's case and it was generally agreed that the town's water supply should be under public control, but again the question was by which institution. The highway board already had powers to supply water for public purposes (e.g. fire-prevention) and had drafted a bill for extending those powers. The Council, however, was promoting the sanitary legislation, and in May 1846 a public meeting was called to resolve the issue. The lively public debate revolved upon the conflict between centralized and diffused authority. Those supporting the highway board cited its long history of public health activity (compared with the Council's lethargy), while those advocating Council control argued the absolute necessity of consolidating power in one body. The highway board's case was considerably weakened by the speech of John A. Tinne, for many years a board member, who supported municipal control because of the frustration he had suffered owing to the divided authority of local government in Liverpool. The majority of speakers commented on the need for amalgamation of powers in the Corporation and the foolishness of perpetuating conflicting and overlapping jurisdictions. The consequence of allowing the highway board to proceed in the light of the Council's impending Sanitary Bill was fruitless duplication of powers, as explained by one Councillor:

> The meeting would at once see the absurdity into which they would be led. . . . The Corporation appointed an inspector of nuisances; the Highway Board would do the same. The Corporation would make bye-laws to regulate courts and passages; the Highway Board would do the same. The Corporation would compel owners to provide privies and ash-pits; the Highway Board would do the same. The Corporation would require notices of alterations in buildings; the Highway Board would do the same. (Great laughter and applause).[9]

It was this line of argument that swamped the highway board, and the meeting agreed on 'the concentration of all power in the hands of the Council, for the more they were entrusted with, the better would they discharge the trust reposed in them.' The 1846 Act was passed on the understanding that a comprehensive plan for water supply would be drawn up by the Council. The 1847 Liverpool Waterworks Act empowered the council to buy out the two companies at the staggering cost of £537,000 and to embark on the famous Rivington scheme.

'Rivington Pike' became for several years the most important issue in Liverpool affairs. Most technical experts whom the Council consulted advised that local sandstone sources could yield no further supplies of water and that water would have to be brought from a distance. A series of linked natural lakes and reservoirs was planned at Rivington Pike near Chorley which would by gravitation feed Liverpool with an abundant and continuous supply of soft water. One of the country's leading civil engineers estimated the total cost of the Rivington scheme at £450,000. Thus with the cost of buying out the two private companies Liverpool Corporation was to enlarge the borough debt by a million pounds. Little wonder that Rivington Pike became a matter of some controversy. The rising tide of concern over the Rivington scheme coincided with the onset of an economic depression in 1848-9 which caused men to question the wisdom of the huge public expenditure involved.

The Council had adopted the original scheme by two votes

in March and April 1847 and the question had been fully aired in the local enquiry arranged by Parliament during the passage of the 1847 Act. It was during 1848 that voices were raised against Rivington and though the municipal elections were fought mainly on the question of whether the docks should be rated, 'the Pike' figured prominently in many contests. Indeed the *Liverpool Mercury*, strongly anti-Pikist, deduced that the 1848 elections necessitated a shelving of the Rivington scheme. In the winter of 1848–9 the anti-Pike propaganda grew to a crescendo. Liverpool was presented with conflicting evidence about the yield and quality of both local and Rivington sources. Statistics abounded which 'proved' that Rivington was unnecessary and that local sources could be exploited at a fraction of the cost of the Pike. The Pike majority survived two hostile motions in November 1848 but had to accept a further enquiry and the appointment of a new and hostile water committee. The high point of the anti-Pike campaign was a crowded and noisy public meeting in February 1849 which voted overwhelmingly against Rivington. Thereafter Pikists were in retreat for the rest of 1849. During the summer the Council formally abandoned Rivington and appointed anti-Pike engineers with a new scheme for local water supply. The November elections were fought solely on the Pike issue which cut right across party lines. Anti-Pikists were victorious and the great champion of sanitary reform Samuel Holme was defeated by a member of his own party.

Anti-Pikists were primarily motivated by economy but this did not mean that they were indifferent to Liverpool's sanitary needs. The Rivington scheme was opposed by many who had the welfare of the townspeople at heart but genuinely believed that Liverpool could be supplied more cheaply by an alternative scheme. This was a dispute between cheap and extravagant social welfare not between social welfare and economy. The point was well made in the *Mercury*:

> The Pikemen would fain make it appear that they only are influenced by sympathies for human suffering and that those who oppose their views are the enemies of the poor and the abettors of pestilence and disease from a niggard spirit of economy. But we contend that those really are the philanthropists who desire to give

to the town an immediate large addition to their supply of pure springwater.[10]

There was an important second point. Much of the argument centred on the just role of the Council. Should it be immune to local opinion? Was it or the community sovereign? From an anti-Pike point of view it appeared that a high handed Council was in need of 'a salutary lesson. It is vain to attempt to ride roughshod over a determined people . . . on any question involving, at a time of great depression, the expenditure of thousands—it may be millions of money.'[11]

The year of anti-Pike progress in 1849 turned out to have a sting in the tail. Not only was the Council legally bound to exercise the powers in the 1847 Act but it had also committed itself to an expenditure of £200,000 by signing contracts in 1847–8. This together with the cost of enlarged local supply would be greater than the cost of the Rivington Scheme. Rivington Pike had become an incubus in which the cost of cancellation outweighed the cost of proceeding. Though anti-Pike political forces were resilient into 1850 they could not resist the conclusion offered by the famous engineer Robert Stephenson:

> I come to the deliberate opinion that, after having expended such large sums of money and incurred such heavy responsibilities to obtain an abundant supply of water of unquestionable quality from an unfailing source by means of gravitation, and consequently at a comparatively inconsiderable annual outlay, the inhabitants of Liverpool would be deserting their true interests, both present and prospective, if they failed to hold fast the powers which they now possess, and may never again be able to obtain, for accomplishing in the most perfect manner, a great social advantage, now so much and so universally sought after . . .[12]

Rivington Pike continued to be a matter of dispute until the water actually flowed into the town in 1857.

In one sense the Rivington contest had weakened the social and political standing of the Corporation in its effects on the social composition of the Council. It would be foolish to say that most Pikists were rich men and most anti-Pikists were poor men. Nevertheless it was true that among the public leaders Pikists included many wealthy merchants and professional men who perhaps took a rather more enlarged view of public affairs. Anti-Pikists, on the other hand, were often shopkeepers or tradesmen for whom, understandably, prospective increases in rates were a serious matter. There was no question that the elections of 1848 and 1849 did dispense with many of the town's elite and the *Mercury* admitted in 1852 that as a result 'the character of the Council became deteriorated; the members ceased to have that influence which was possessed by their predecessors and gentlemen thought it no longer an honour to have a seat in our Council Chamber.' In a more fundamental sense, however, Rivington strengthened the hand of the Council. Rivington Pike was a monument to civil engineering: it was also a great tribute to municipal enterprise. The Council had emerged successfully through a baptism of fire by providing for the community's welfare, almost despite itself. Municipal reform had defined its purpose through public health.

THE COUNCIL AS SANITARY REFORMER

The 1846 Sanitary Act gave Liverpool an almost unique opportunity to demonstrate the role of municipal government as protector of the public health. Duncan, as M.O.H., had a traumatic apprenticeship as he faced the triple challenge of massive Irish immigration because of famine, an economic depression and a cholera epidemic (Frazer, 1947, 56-63). In the short term he faced only crisis as death rates soared in 1847, as high as 135 per thousand in Vauxhall Ward, due to fever (typhoid and typhus) and diarrhoea (dysentry). Two years later the cholera epidemic of 1849 pushed the city's death rate up to 52 per thousand. Though lacking the medical and scientific knowledge to understand the nature of the endemic and epidemic diseases which so afflicted Liverpool, Duncan was nevertheless able to direct the Corporation towards the right environmental solutions — cleansing of the streets, drainage, sewerage, inspection of health hazards, the clearing of the cellars. Already by 1849 Duncan's educative role was paying dividends and John Tinne, chairman of the health committee, laid down a bold programme of objectives:

> The substitution of water closets for privies, the abolition of cesspools, the banishment of all noxious manufactures from the vicinity of inhabited places, the removal of slaughterhouses without the borough, the total prevention of intra-mural interments;—these with an abundant supply of water, the due apportionment of population to area, the widening of streets, the establishing of well-regulated Abbatoirs beyond the precincts of the borough.[13]

Such a programme indicates the extent to which the Corporation of Liverpool had already acknowledged a responsibility for the environmental welfare of the community, with a consequent willingness to interfere with the free exercise of property rights. Public health reform rested on the triple pillars of the cleansing and drainage of the streets, sewerage and water supply. Rivington made the other two possible. As the borough engineer James Newlands explained in 1858;

> There is the great blessing of immensely increased supply of water laid on in every house, and as a result of this, an increase of baths in private houses of moderate rental, the extension of the use of water closets and the gradual abandoning of cesspools. This increased water supply, too, permits the thorough periodic flushing of the sewers and drains, the washing of courts and passages and the proper watering of the streets.[14]

Newlands himself had drawn up a comprehensive plan for drainage and sewerage in 1848 which the Council had adopted and ten years later he was able to ascertain the progress made. About eighty miles of sewers had been constructed including a main outlet sewer which was the largest in the country, some six miles in length and six feet high by four feet wide. A further sixty-six miles of main street drains had been built and the total cost of all drains and sewers had been over £215,000. Nearly £200,000 had been spent on paving of new and existing streets and in 1858 over three hundred scavengers were employed on street cleansing (Newlands, 1859). It was estimated that a total of over £3m. had been expended by the corporation since the passing of the 1846 Act.*

Newlands freely acknowledged that such physical improvements did not produce spectacular or immediate results, yet another corporation official could cite real progress as a result of public health reform (McGowen, 1859, 15-30). There had been a substantial fall in the death rate which Duncan estimated at a saving of over 3,000 lives per annum in the late 1850s. In the most vital of all vital statistics, municipal public health reform was thus advancing public welfare. There had also been, it was claimed, a cumulative improvement in morality and behaviour which stemmed from the amelioration in housing conditions. There were those, however, who believed that the costs of such improvements, running into millions, outweighed the benefits. In Liverpool, as elsewhere, ratepayer associations grew up aiming to control local expenditure and keep rates down. In 1851 such 'economist' groups were flourishing with ward committees and their own newspaper, *The Liverpool Burgess and Ratepayers' Magazine*, which lashed the Corporation for its extravagance. 'Economy' never fully dominated the Liverpool scene partly because of the subsidies to ratepayers accruing from the vast corporate estate, valued at £4m. in 1853. Not only had important capital projects been financed by this 'municipal cornucopia,' current expenditure was also subsidized to the tune of £60,000 per annum or a shilling in the pound on the rates. The Liverpool burgess was thus somewhat insulated from the real costs of local improvement.

Perhaps because of this, the 1850s were a decade of ambitious plans and growing public expenditure. J. A. Picton, later Liverpool's foremost antiquarian, proposed a massive scheme of street development and public adornment which would 'rival Athens, Rome or Munich in beauty and magnificence.' He wanted wider thoroughfares and an extended transport system to serve the town's commercial needs but also proposed slum clearance via 'the projection of new

---

*Capital and recurrent expenditure 1847-58 comprised; Sanitary works £1.3m., Waterworks £1.6m., lighting and watching £0.7m., Other (inc., baths, libraries, parks etc.,) £0.1m. Total £3.7m.

lines of streets through the densely peopled and squalid districts, bearing health and salubrity to the abodes of disease, and converting the foulest blot on the town's escutcheon into a means of usefulness and ornament' (Picton, 1853, 10). Now was the time to defend the town's honour against Chadwick's gibes. The great sanitary reformer had pilloried Liverpool for building the splendid St. George's Hall while ignoring sanitation, but a local worthy (Baines, 1852, 677) could now cite sewerage, cleansing, baths and wash-houses, housing reform and water supply in reply. Given the Irish problem it was doubtful if Liverpool could ever be a really healthy town 'but it would be a great injustice to suppose that the people of Liverpool are erecting magnificent buildings and leaving the poor to perish.' And it was the Council which was at the centre of this new dimension in local administration.

Yet what was later termed 'a period of boasting' turned out to have been premature and it was truly remarked that in the light of subsequent events 'all must surely regret the boasted sanitary progress of Liverpool which was then made' (Shimmin 1866, 14). The self-congratulation of the 1850s was followed by renewed concern and puzzlement in the 1860s as death rates rose once more. The resurgence of typhus in 1865 and the fourth visitation of cholera in 1866 pushed the death rate up to 50 per thousand at its peak. Like the return of some outmoded fashion, the whole sanitary crusade had to be begun again.

Ironically part of the problem originated in the earlier sanitary history of the town. Perhaps the most prominent sources of disease identified in the 1840s were the cellars of Liverpool, notorious even in the national public health campaign. Under the 1842 Building Act and the 1846 Sanitation Act the Council introduced regulations on the minimum size of dwellings and consequently acquired powers (confirmed in the 1854 Sanitary Amendment Act) to clear the cellars. Public health reformers were proud of their achievement in clearing perhaps 8,000 cellars between the early 1840s and the mid-1850s, yet other than staggering the evictions from cellars in order to avoid swamping the housing market nothing was done to cater for the housing needs of those summarily evicted. It must not be forgotten that no town in England had such a high proportion of its labour force engaged in casual work. Irregular employment and much migration created a demand for the poorest accommodation. When incomes were low and intermittent, it was natural that desperately poor tenants, flushed out of the cellars, would be driven into the courts and alleys to live. The Liverpool courts were scarcely more salubrious than the cellars, and the cramming of ever more occupiers into these cramped quarters generated a major health hazard. These courts and alleys were invariably *culs-de-sac* without access to light and air, and they were soon infested with open sewers and cesspools. It was common to find a putrefying cesspool at the entrance through which both people and air would have to pass to enter the close confines within.

It is one of the truisms of the history of public health that nuisances had to be put under people's very noses before the public was aware of sanitary problems. Residential zoning removed middle-class property owners from the scenes of squalor and it was literally the case that sanitary evils often were not seen by the middle class. Furthermore Liverpool's sanitary code, with its health committee, medical officer and nuisance inspectors, encouraged a public assumption that the Council had these things well under control. Thus when death rates increased again in he 1860s it was as necessary as ever for the sanitary crusader to force the public to take note of the environmental disaster of the courts and alleys. That public opinion engendered action was largely the result of the campaign of a prolific local author, Hugh Shimmin, who shamed Liverpool out of its lethargy.

Shimmin wrote a series of articles in 1863 on Liverpool's courts and alleys which appeared in *Porcupine*, a relatively new weekly periodical which irreverently explored municipal and parochial affairs in the town. Such journals may have been common at this period, for *Porcupine* was identical in format, style and appearance to the *Town Crier* in Birmingham. Both journals concentrated in a satirical style on municipal affairs. As this journal proudly claimed, 'to *Porcupine* belongs the exclusive merit of having rivetted public attention to this subject.' Shimmin's descriptions were so horrific that many critics, ignorant of the real condition of the courts and alleys, accused him of exaggeration. Yet he held his course until the Council agreed to take action and open up the courts. Such a result was achieved by

> the reiteration of descriptions, many of which seemed even gross, but their truthfulness being at last recognised that very grossness became a power. The nuisance was, as it were, *held under the nostrils of the town*, till the Town Council was compelled by public disgust to abolish it.[15]

It is important at this point to amend the description of Liverpool municipal affairs in the 1860s which has previously been purveyed. White (1951) makes no mention of this campaign to mobilize opinion while claiming that municipal politics in the 1860s were devoid of public interest, without party contests, and that Conservatives were comfortably in control of the Council. In fact in the 1860s municipal politics were brought to a new level of intensity, as radical Liberals made a concerted push to gain municipal power. In 1863 a Liberal mayor was elected and in the decade from 1858 there was only one year when the Liberals did not have at least half of the elected seats in the Council. In short, the maintenance of Tory rule was dependent upon their monopoly of the aldermanic seats. Far from being a period of municipal quiescence, the early 1860s were marked by an interest in Council matters, as witnessed by the 1861 launching of *Porcupine*, which immediately became a thriving municipal journal. Shimmin's campaign on the courts and the radical thrust in local elections coalesced in the 1863 ward contests when the leader of the municipal reformers, Joseph Robinson, made the opening up of the courts the main plank in his election campaign. Indeed when one of the Rathbones, traditional leaders of Liverpool's elite Whigs, couched his election address in broad philosophical terms about the nature and history of municipal government, he was roundly criticized. Electors wanted to know

> something about the landing-stage approaches and the paving of the streets and the cleansing of the courts. We do not want any reflections upon the origins of municipal government; we rather

desire to hear how municipal government in Liverpool means to spend our rates, supply our water and cleanse our sewers.[16]

Sanitary reform had become the stuff of municipal politics.

As a result of the mobilization of opinion both the Health Committee and the full Council had agreed to seek new powers to deal with the courts and alleys, yet Shimmin did not rest his case. His articles together with supplementary comment were published as a pamphlet, *The Courts and Alleys of Liverpool* (1864), which sustained the sanitary crusade. Shimmin acknowledged the valuable work done by religious philanthropists, for instance in the ragged school movement, but he maintained that a more fundamental moral teaching was required:

> Whilst in no way disparaging the efforts of zealous men who are striving to 'evangelize the masses' we contend that the religion needed most in the 'Little Hells' of Liverpool is, the 'Religion of Newlands'—good paving, enforced cleanliness, and plenty of light.[17]

Stimulated by public opinion the Council successfully sponsored a new and far-reaching local bill, the Liverpool Sanitary Amendment Act of 1864, which endowed the Corporation with more powers than any other authority in England. By this Act the M.O.H. was empowered to identify, and if necessary condemn, houses unfit for habitation; and the Council, by virtue of loans of up to £100,000 and a one penny rate, was enabled to purchase and demolish houses so designated. By the end of the century some 5,000 houses had been demolished under this scheme. The Health Committee had frequently been clamped between the opposing views of sanitary reformers, who wished to light and ventilate working-class dwellings so that they were more conducive to health, and cottage owners who wished to cram the largest number of dwellings on the smallest space. The 1864 Act firmly tilted the balance against property owners and strengthened the sanitary arm of the Corporation.

The Act was a consequence of public concern which had been aroused by Shimmin and the *Porcupine*. Yet the campaign would not have borne fruit without the active support of not only Council representatives but also of Council officials, pre-eminent among whom was James Newlands, the borough engineer. It was he who kept the Council plodding along the hard sanitary road, and *Porcupine* rather selflessly described him as 'the be all and end all of the new Sanitary Improvement Act which introduced a new and prolific principle into social legislation.' Expectations of the beneficial results of the Act rested on both its environmental and its moral effects, for the Council had great opportunity to adopt the role of sanitary teacher:

> It is the duty of the authorities, when they find people so ignorant in regard to cleanliness and housekeeping to do all in their power to instruct them. The court and alley inspectors, if rightly trained for their work and fully alive to the importance of it, ought to act as schoolmasters to bring the poor to cleanliness. Rightly viewed, all the inspectors under the health acts are educational officers.[18]

This assault upon the courts was accompanied by a renewed attack upon another pernicious health hazard, the tunnel midden system. The public outcry on the courts coincided with Dr. W. S. Trench's first annual report as Minister of Health (having succeeded Duncan in 1863) in which he identified the tunnel middens of human excrement as the main cause of persistent high death rates. People were thus always living in close proximity to the sources of disease. Hence the opening up of the courts went hand in hand with the removal of the middens and renewed pressure to convert houses to the water closet system. Just as some property owners resisted the improvements of the courts, so many of them opposed the conversion to a water borne sewerage system. Indeed this apparently minor question generated great political passion for 'the advocates of the dry earth system and the fluid method of deodorisation fight as bitterly as did the partisans of the Neptunian against the Vulcanian philosophers who theorized upon the original formation of the world.'[19]

REACTION AND THE RESURGENCE
OF THE MUNICIPAL IDEAL

Both the courts and the middens were resistent to improvement and it took a long time before public health reform yielded real dividends in the saving of life. In the 1860s the crude death rate in Liverpool borough averaged over 33 per thousand and there was particularly high infant mortality. One in four babies did not live to see first birthdays. In the 1870s the death rate fell to 29.5, but this was still very high (and higher than most other large towns). Figures for Liverpool parish (i.e. excluding the outlying townships) were even higher, during the 1860s 39 per thousand, in the 1870s nearly 34 per thousand. By the end of the century the death rate had fallen to about 25 per thousand, a vast improvement on mid-Victorian Liverpool but still alarmingly high when the national figure was around 18. Moreover, it would be wrong to think of Liverpool Corporation as working steadily and ever more successfully in the sanitary field. Municipal energy was an intermittent variable, and public health reform moved in fits and starts. As elsewhere, public enthusiasm alternated with public apathy. The initial interest and activity of the 1840s was sustained into the early 1850s, when there followed a time of resting on laurels. Concern revived in the early 1860s, but by the end of decade a reaction had set in and by 1869 some of the borrowing powers in the 1864 Act had been allowed to lapse. Indeed in the late Victorian years a more fundamental conservatism established itself which transformed Liverpool Council from a pioneering authority into one immobilized by inertia. Early and mid-Victorian Liverpool led the nation in sanitary reform but often late Victorian Liverpool had to be prodded into action by government order.

Much of the reason for this flowed from a fundamental change in the financial position of Liverpool Corporation which gradually worked itself out in the later Victorian years. In 1857, after a history of complaint and squabbling over whether the docks should be rated, Liverpool Corporation lost control of the dock estate, receiving £1.5m in compensation for the loss of town dues which the Council had previously levied. The Mersey Docks and Harbour Board henceforward administered the docks of the port of Liverpool. Though the residue of the corporate estate was still substantial, it meant that the Council would become more dependent upon rates to finance municipal expenditure. Increased rates inevitably aroused public hostility, particularly among less wealthy burgesses for whom rates represented a substantial financial burden. William Rathbone, M.P. for Liverpool from 1868 to 1880, explained how the town's rating system favoured the wealthy. He calculated that a merchant and ship-owner might be assessed at 1 per cent of his income, a young doctor at 2 per cent, a labourer at 4 per cent and a tradesman at 12 per cent (Rathbone, 1908, 238). Understandably 'Municipal Economy' became a popular electoral slogan among many ratepayers; and the Land and Houseowners' Association, first launched at the end of the 1850s, flourished in the late 1860s and early 1870s, acting as a brake upon municipal progress.

Nothing exemplified the change of atmosphere more clearly than a series of open letters written by Samuel Holme in 1870 which appeared in the *Liverpool Courier*. It will be recalled that Holme had been one of the pioneers of sanitary reform in the 1840s. Indeed his municipal career spanned the years of great expansion in corporate functions, for he had entered the Council in 1842 when it had just obtained the Health of the Town Act, and he had retired in 1864 when the Council acquired its new powers under the Sanitary Amendment Act. In 1870 Holme took on the role of municipal elder statesman, warning against excessive expenditure. He criticized the Finance Committee's lack of control over corporate expenditure, the Health Committee's wayward extravagance and the whole Council's pernicious adoption of too many responsibilities. That Holme should advocate retrenchment was a blow to municipal reformers, and the 1870s were thus a time of consolidation and maintenance of the *status quo* rather than of positive new departures in municipal policy. Holme's was by no means a lone voice. Rathbone, himself an advocate of effective local administration, confirmed that

> the amount of local taxation and of local indebtedness had increased with startling rapidity . . . the weight of taxation laid

by local bodies on the present generation was serious but what mattered far more was their unlimited power of burdening with debt the industry of the future.[20]

Such views reached a peak in Liverpool in the early 1880s. The town's renewed search for water had led to the ambitious Vyrnwy scheme, and this was for late Victorian Liverpool what Rivington Pike had been for the early Victorian years — an issue of great financial and political controversy. For municipal 'economists' Vyrnwy's two million pounds was the final straw, and a campaign for municipal retrenchment was launched which effectively halted improvement in Liverpool. Emulating Shimmin, John Lovell used the press to stimulate public feeling, but this time against and not in favour of municipal endeavour. In 1884–5 the *Liverpool Mercury* ran a series of twelve articles by Lovell on the subject of municipal government in the town. These went much further than previous bouts of municipal economy by claiming that there had been not only extravagance and inefficiency in local administration but also corruption in the mysterious disappearance of corporate profits into the municipal estate. In particular Lovell attacked the corporate estate which had been doubly pernicious in its effects: it had encouraged a spirit of public largesse, and because it was inefficiently administered, it had actually cost the ratepayers millions of pounds. In forthright terms Lovell proclaimed, 'it is the white elephant of municipal Liverpool. For every pound which the estate has contributed towards the ordinary expenses of local government, it has taken thirty shillings out of the pockets of the ratepayers'. Lovell lashed out at the gross inefficiency of the municipal water supply and the wanton extravagance of improvement schemes. His articles appeared as a ninety-page pamphlet that emphasized the net effects of this municipal dissipation in high rates. Of Lovell's many statistics, His most compelling were those which demonstrated that, while the population had increased by 50 per cent and the rateable value by 112 per cent between 1851 and 1883, rates in the pound had increased by 270 per cent and rates per capita by a staggering 442 per cent. (Lovell, 1885, 32.)

Superficially it appeared that the popular resistance of the 1870s had not had the desired effect, for improvement schemes had continued the merry dance started in 1858. Indeed, as Lovell explained, a total expenditure of nearly three million pounds had been authorized by nine local acts between 1858 and 1883.* This was, however, somewhat deceptive, since the loan powers were not always exercised, much of the money was for the purchase of parks, and some of the street improvements were geared more to the commercial than to the sanitary needs of the town. Even in this sphere 'the flood of improvements of the sixties dwindled to a trickle in the seventies and dried up altogether after 1883.' (White, 1951, 85). More significantly, it was just in the areas of positive provision for groups in need that Liverpool Council was most reluctant to act. In the quarter century from 1870, when there was a growing understanding of poverty and a realization of the limited effects of mere environmental control, Liverpool was effectively paralysed by municipal economists and traditional individualist ideas.

Hospital and housing provision well illustrate the point. From an early point in the sanitary history of the town, medical opinion recognized the need to isolate infection in times of epidemic, and both in 1847 and 1864–6 it was suggested that the Council should provide hospitals. The Council declined to do so and the only public hospital provision was that provided through the Poor Law by the Select Vestry. National legislation in both 1866 and 1872 empowered the Corporation to provide hospitals, but the Council chose not to exercise such powers. The Council dutifully followed the advice of Trench as M.O.H., who, though concerned with high morbidity and mortality rates, asserted in his 1871 annual report that the Council could not provide hospitals 'without expense and the manifest waste of public funds' and advised the Council not to 'undertake

---

*The details of each act are as follows; 1858, £130,000; 1861, £130,000; 1864, £300,000; 1865, £700,000; 1867, £850,000; 1871, £185,000; 1878, £125,000; 1882, £146,000; 1883, £35,000. Total expenditure authorized £2,916,000.

responsibilities which are foreign to their usual duties.' Disinclined to adopt new functions, the Council was sharply rebuked by the Local Government Board in both 1883 and 1885 for failing to fulfil hospital responsibilities laid on corporations by national legislation. Only reluctantly, and then with much prevarication, did Liverpool Council grudgingly acknowledge its responsibilities in this field after 1885, and it was not until 1898 that it voted to build an entirely new hospital.

Hospital provision was a natural corollary of sanitary reform and so too was housing. The clearing of the cellars then of the courts and the emphasis upon overcrowding led inevitably to the question of the public supply of cheap housing. Influential opinion was, however, hostile to such a novel idea. Thus two distinguished doctors, reporting in 1871 on Liverpool's persistently high death rate, concluded that 'surface overcrowding' bred 'the barbarous habits of a half-civilized race' and identified the remedy in dispersal of population through increased housing supply away from the insanitary areas. Nevertheless, they pronounced, 'it is impossible for the Corporation to provide houses for its poor citizens—that would simply be offering a premium to pauperism.' (Parkes and Sanderson, 1871, 76.) Perhaps the best contemporary statement of the case against municipal housing came from a philanthropist who was searching for the best way of providing cheap accommodation for casual labourers. He laid down clear limits to corporate functions:

> it is the duty of local authorities to provide a sufficient supply of pure water-efficient sewerage—and convenient streets, kept in a cleanly condition,—and to prevent nuisances. These are necessaries for the inhabitants in common; but it would scarcely be suggested that it is the duty of a corporation to find all the inhabitants with houses. If it is not so, it does not appear to be consistent with sound policy that they should provide dwellings for a portion of them. The ordinary capitalist . . . is placed at a disadvantage, and unfairly so by corporations entering into competition with him . . . and the tendency of unequal or unfair competition is always to discourage capital from being invested in the enterprise . . . it does not appear justifiable for municipal authorities to build labourers' dwellings.[21]

The dictates of free competition and municipal economy restricted the Council's housing activities. Its pioneering experiment of building St. Martin's Cottages in 1869 remained for many years an isolated model of corporation housing. Victoria Buildings followed in 1885 but it was not until 1895 that a Council Committee on insanitary property recommended that corporation houses be provided for those displaced as a result of the Council's slum clearance programme. From 1900 the Council had a Housing Committee which by 1914 had built nearly 2,400 houses to add to the 500 provided before the turn of the century.

This more positive approach mirrored other areas of municipal endeavour, for the swing of the pendulum again pushed the Council into new fields. The decade or so from 1895 (when the Conservatives regained power after three years of Liberal rule) was a period of renewed enthusiasm and activity, as Liverpool became once more a pioneering municipality. The growing political importance of organized labour, which focused attention on the needs of the working class, the emergence of a socially aware Conservatism which followed the ideas of the housing reformer Sir Arthur Forwood, and developments in national ideas and policy combined to increase the pace and extent of municipal involvement after 1895. The community as a whole was the recipient of municipal services, with electricity and transport added to water supply, and those in need were being aided in such fields as education and welfare under both local and national legislation.

Nobody had yet coined the phrase 'welfare state,' but by the early years of the twentieth century a local historian was able to identify the Liverpool corporation as an agency for 'cradle to grave' welfare:

> It offers to see that the child is brought safely into the world. It provides him in infancy with suitable food. It gives him playgrounds to amuse himself in and baths to swim in. It takes him to school . . . it trains him for his future trade. It sees that the citizen's house is properly built and sometimes even builds it for him. It brings into his rooms an unfailing supply of pure water from the remote hills. It guards his food and tries to secure that it

is not dangerously adulterated. It sweeps the streets for him and disposes of the refuse of his house. It carries him swiftly to and from his work. It gives him books to read, pictures to look at, music to listen to and lectures to stimulate his thought. If he is sick it nurses him; if he is penniless it houses him; and when he dies, if none other will, it buries him.[22]

It was all so very different from 1835, when little more than judicial functions were envisaged and all so unexpected when corporations were viewed as merely private bodies with some public duties. The route from the limited corporation of the 1830s to the welfare agency of the early twentieth century had by no means been straight and narrow, for the journey of varying pace had been tortuous, encompassing troughs and peaks. Yet one thing was clear. The long march that terminated in a form of 'municipal socialism' had begun when the Council adopted responsibility for the environmental health of the local community, and it was continued into unexplored regions when the Corporation acknowledged a wider definition of municipal welfare.

Three
Leeds

THE IMPACT OF MUNICIPAL REFORM

Leeds, unlike Manchester and Birmingham, with which it is often compared, was a corporate town long before the industrial revolution. Its commercial importance in the West Riding wool trade was recognized in the grant of a charter of incorporation in 1626, confirmed and re-issued in 1661. In both charters the members of the Corporation are named and they were for the most part wealthy merchants involved in the purchase and sale of woollen cloth. The Leeds Corporation was indeed the formal expression of the local control of an oligarchy of 'gentlemen merchants' (Wilson, 1971, Chap. I). Under the aegis of this commercial elite, though hardly because of its corporate activities, the town prospered, and by the early nineteenth century was both an industrial and mercantile metropolis. The Corporation dutifully nodded towards the industrial revolution by elevating to corporate office a few cloth manufacturers (as distinct from merchants) and a sprinkling of representatives of the town's newer trades such as flax spinning and engineering. But it was ill-fitted to respond in any more positive way to the challenge of industrialization.

On the eve of municipal reform the major indictment of the Leeds Corporation was its exclusiveness, the characteristic defect of the old regime as a whole. In terms similar to those used elsewhere the Corporation Commissioners recorded:

> The close constitution of the corporation is obvious; all vacancies in each branch of it being filled by the Select Body gives to that body absolute and uncontrolled self-election. Family influence is predominant. Fathers and sons and sons-in-law, brothers and

brothers-in-law succeed to the offices of the corporation like matters of family settlement.[1]

When local reformers were inclined to be charitable to the Corporation because of its relative purity, Edward Baines, the politically active editor of the Liberal *Leeds Mercury*, sharply reminded Whigs and Dissenters that it was 'characterized by the most rigourous exclusion of all persons differing in politics or religious creed from the favoured few.' The Leeds Corporation was a Tory Anglican preserve and this was crucial, for, as the Webbs explained, 'it was not the administrative inefficiency or the failure in honesty that brought down the local oligarchies but above all their exclusiveness.'[2] In Leeds, the Commissioners noted, the consequence of this exclusiveness was the politicizing of improvement commissions and vestry, where the political opponents of the Corporation created a rival focus of political authority in the town. A popularly elected Liberal vestry and commission acted as a counterweight to a self-elected Tory Corporation.

Yet Leeds Corporation had one redeeming feature — its poverty. It was one of the purest because it was one of the poorest Corporations. Whereas Liverpool Corporation had an annual income of £90,000, in Leeds a paltry £220 per annum accrued from the small corporate investments. Without great wealth for corruption and without a parliamentary constituency to corrupt (Leeds was not enfranchised until 1832), the exclusiveness of Leeds Corporation was tempered by its impotence. It lacked the means and the setting for the exercise of its proscriptive influence. This was symptomatic of the corporation's lack of functions. It presided over, but did not cater for, the town. Its essential character was revealingly portrayed when its bye laws were codified in 1823 (Wardell, 1846, 90). The by-laws, the corporation stated, 'were made and settled for the due ordering, good government and welfare of this corporation': modern by-laws exist for the good government and welfare of the *community*. The corporation existed as a private institution with no responsibility for the interests of the town and such social utilities as were provided for the convenience and welfare of the citizens emanated from non-municipal bodies, the vestry, the improvement commission, the highway surveyors.

In the administration of justice, however, the corporation had a good record and contemporaries spoke well of its respectability. Parliamentary Commissioners reported in 1833 'every person whom we consulted agreed so remarkably in eulogising the present corporation of Leeds that we cannot doubt that the town is well governed through their means' while the Corporation Commission confirmed that 'the great respectability of the present members of the corporation and their impartial conduct as justices were universally acknowledged.'[3] It was therefore with some justification that the unreformed Corporation of Leeds recorded a protest against municipal reform.

> The Leeds Corporation has been proved free from all taint of corruption and malversation and the magistracy appointed under its charter has ever performed its duties honestly fearlessly and independently to the satisfaction of the inhabitants at large, this Court therefore feels it a duty to record its sense of the unjust judgment by which this Corporation is included in the condemnation passed on Corporations generally.[4]

Unjust or not, the verdict passed on the unreformed system ended the life of Leeds Corporation. The first municipal election in December 1835 was an abject defeat for the traditional governors of the town, with the Liberals winning 42 of the 48 Council seats. Even after the victors charitably provided the Conservatives with four aldermanic seats the Council was weighted 51–13 in favour of the Liberals. It was as Baines explained 'a transference of local power beyond all calculations.' Embittered Tories sneered at the alleged social inferiority of the new rulers, 'political mountebanks, bankrupt tradesmen and potato carriers' and at an early election a member of the old elite complained

> I hope the time is not far distant when we shall again have something like order—when rank and station, education and moral worth, will resume their proper place in society, when innkeepers and tradesmen will be content to allow those who are more justly entitled to hold all offices of trust and power.[5]

It is now clear (Hennock, 1973, 185) that these fears about the social quality of the new Council were premature. There was no great difference between the social composition of the Corporation and the Council: the same sort of professions and occupations dominated both. The fundamental difference lay in politics, religion and family history. The Town Council was controlled by the alternative elite of Leeds, Liberal in politics, for the most part Nonconformist in religion and relatively recent arrivals. The old oligarchy comprised a network of well established local Tory-Anglican families: the new regime centred on Liberal Dissenters whose antecedents often lay outside the town.

Permanent outsiders became insiders and the newcomers revelled in the exercise of power. As a local Whig aristocrat put it, the Liberals were now 'sharing in the first fruits of that system in all possible prosperity and credit.' When considering the early years of the Leeds Council, it is interesting to note the comments of two great admirers of the English system (Redlich and Hirst, 1903, I, 276) who asserted 'a municipal spoils system in England is almost unthinkable.' Yet such a system certainly existed in Leeds in the early years of municipal reform. Corporate posts, the town clerk, the clerk of the peace, the recorder, went to Liberal activists; corporate contracts such as printing were awarded to Liberal sympathizers; and the corporate offices of alderman mayor and magistrate were distributed on a strictly party basis. Well might the expelled elite cynically note that the great complaint of the old system, its political exclusiveness, applied with equal force to the new. Liberal motives in supporting municipal reform were now seen to be a desire 'to finger the public money,' for, as an indignant Tory complained, they 'grasp at every possible thing in the shape of profit or power with the most unblushing inconsistency . . . solely aiming at party monopoly and personal aggrandisement.'[6] Baines, the Liberal spokesman, offered an all embracing defence to this mode of attack—previous proscription required belated correction:

> Almost everywhere the Lord Lieutenants, the County Magistrates, the Clergy, the Police, the functionaries of our law courts from the

Judges on the Bench to the humblest officer and all the endless train of dependants on each, including the publicans, the *employés* of the Corporations etc., have within living memory been of the Tory party.[7]

The Liberal elation at the exercise of power was soon checked when it was discovered that the old Corporation had alienated all funds lest they fall into the hands of the new political masters. The sums were modest but the significance great. Through fines levied on those who refused to serve in corporate office, the old regime had accumulated £7,000 which had been invested, £6,500 in government stock and £500 in the Leeds and Wakefield turnpike trust. It was from these investments that the Corporation had derived its small income. In May 1835 the Corporation resolved to rid itself of these funds by vesting control in a small trust which would expend the money on Anglican Churches and charities. The disposition of the funds was the subject of clear corporate instructions, whose purpose was to deprive the new Council of its inheritance. The last item in the accounts of the trust fund reads 'To the Treasurer of the National School £34-8s-1d': on 26 December, 1835 the very last penny of the borough fund was spent. The Council property in 1836 thus comprised not £7,000 as anticipated but a mace and a few pews in Leeds Parish Church.

The alienation of the borough fund was regarded by municipal reformers as a deliberate blow at the authority of the Town Council, whose dignity was thereby impugned. It was immediately agreed to begin legal proceedings for the restoration of corporate property and this Chancery suit became a symbolic battle between old and new forms of local government. The case was a vital one for Leeds as was the more celebrated *Rutter v Chapman** for Manchester. Both

---

*This was a test case where the Lancashire County Coroner challenged the right of the newly appointed Borough Coroner to hold inquests in Manchester. It tested whether the new Corporation of Manchester could legally appoint a coroner. Hence it tested whether the Manchester Charter was legal.

called into question the legal standing and moral authority of the new Town Councils. Both had to be won if the fruits of municipal reform were to be gathered.

In Leeds the case became a political football booted around Council chamber, public meeting and newspaper press for five years. In propagandist, though not in legal terms, the question turned on the nature of the funds — was this public or private property? The Tory case, re-iterated *ad nauseam*, was that the money had derived solely from private individuals paying fines to the old Corporation and not in any sense from the public at large. As one Tory angrily expressed it,

> Neither the Liberals nor theirs, nor the township nor the parish, nor the public, nor any charitable grant, devise or bequest whatsoever contributed a single sixpence: there is not one dissenting farthing amongst it. It was contributed entirely by the Corporators and for the Corporators.[8]

This line of argument was rejected by municipal reformers who insisted that the money was public property and was specifically covered by the Municipal Reform Act by which corporate funds must pass to the new councils. In some places the alienation of funds had been accompanied by personal corruption but members of the Leeds Corporation were not charged with peculation. This left the field of accusation wide open:

> We do deliberately charge them with *breach of trust* to the Borough, with a *gross misappropriation of public property* — with a distribution of funds as unfair as it was *wrongful* — with a palpable attempt to *evade the law* — with an *unworthy and disreputable trick* — and with a *flagrant insult* towards the *New Corporation* and towards the *Burgess* whom the Corporation represent.[9]

Where one side saw the alienation as the robbery of the burgesses and the Chancery suit as the restitution of public property, the other saw legitimate private expenditure and the robbery of the charities.

In a matter so vital to the interests of municipal reform a speedy judgement was desired but there were frustrating delays. Liberal encouragement at receiving the initial support of the Attorney-General, whose authority was needed to proceed in this public case, was dampened by slow legal process and deliberate prevarication. Witnesses from the old Corporation refused to give evidence or to produce documents without compulsion from the courts so that every stage was protracted. Though strengthened in their resolve by an initial judgement in November 1837 rejecting the defendants' plea that there was no *prima facie* case to answer, Liberal councillors were somewhat demoralized to find that when the case was finally set down for a hearing in February 1839 there were four to five hundred cases ahead of it. By September 1840, legal costs of proceedings were already £1,459 and the case had not yet been heard.

These delays were especially worrying, since Tory strength on the Council was growing and the obstructive tactics of the defendants derived partly from the hope that the Liberals would lose their majority and the Chancery suit would be dropped. There were regular motions for abandoning the case and one of these in 1839 was lost by only a single vote. The upsurge of municipal Toryism may be gauged from Table 1.

Table 3.1   *Political Composition of Leeds Town Council 1835–41*

	Councillors		Aldermen		Whole Council	
	Liberal	Tory	Liberal	Tory	Liberal	Tory
1835–6	39	9	12	4	51	13
1836–7	37	11	12	4	49	15
1837–8	33	15	12	4	45	19
1838–9	27	21	16	0	43	21
1839–40	20	28	16	0	36	28
1840–41	16	32	16	0	32	32

By 1839, the majority of councillors were Tory and during 1840–1 the Council was balanced on a knife edge, with the aldermanic bench alone preventing Tory control. A general pro-Tory swing, superior registration activity, economic depression and increased municipal expenditure explain this electoral success. Desperate reformers, after the November 1840 elections had failed to reverse the anti-Liberal trend, probably through local Whig M.P.'s, persuaded the Lord Chancellor, to expedite the Chancery suit which was finally heard in December 1840.

The decision wholly vindicated the Council's position and the money had to be repaid, together with costs. When the final accounts were rendered, it emerged that the borough fund had to bear a net outlay of £803 in order to recover stock worth £6,183. Yet the financial settlement was less important than the psychological boost given to municipal reform in Leeds. The authority of the new Council had been confirmed, its dignity acknowledged and its status enhanced. The Leeds Town Council had emerged from the shadow of the unreformed Corporation. An uncertain Municipal apprenticeship had been successfully completed.

SANITARY REFORM

But what did that add up to? If Walmsley had asked his question 'What Have The Council Done?' in Leeds instead of Liverpool, what would the answer have been after the Council's legal vindication? Part of the reply would have involved those same general principles which appealed to all municipal reformers. The Council was now popularly elected where the Corporation had been self-elected so that citizens were now free agents in municipal matters instead of under the tutelage of a municipal oligarchy. All suspicion of financial malpractice was removed by the device of annual accounts and strict budgetary control. Publicity acted as the watchdog of the municipality as Council proceedings were now open. Beyond these almost philosophical improvements, the practical consequences of municipal reform were more difficult to discern. There was one important current expenditure and one capital project which the new Council could point to, a new police force and Armley gaol, which says much of the priorities and functions of Leeds Town Council.

The one compulsory committee which Councils were forced to have was the Watch Committee and one of the earliest tasks of the Leeds Council was the reform of the borough police force. The day and night forces were amalgamated and the former enlarged. New blue uniforms were purchased and this caught the public imagination as a cause of increased municipal expenditure. It has recently been argued (Storch, 1975) that the daily surveillance of working-class areas was a prime function of the new urban police forces, but many contemporaries could see no use for 'the day parades of dandy policemen';

> The streets have been studded with an idle day police the main performance of which is the payment of abject homage to their Whig-Radical creators by the salute military as they pass along. On foolish frippery of this sort it is that the public money is squandered.[10]

Police expenditure was resented on all sides. A Tory councillor, complaining of the size of the force, believed that 'Leeds was a quiet inland town' while a Radical, scorning talk of a Chartist riot as an excuse for extra police, remarked 'all this talk about Chartism reminded him of Billy Pitt who when he wanted to increase the army was continually telling the country that Bonaparte was expected in England every day.'

Many of those who wished to economize on police expenditure were also anxious to reverse the decision to build Armley Gaol, ironically the first example of Leeds civic pride. It was befitting the dignity of a town the size of Leeds to have its own gaol, rather than maintain its rather servile dependence upon the West Riding prison authorities at Wakefield. The decision to build a Leeds prison was made by the Council in November 1837, but in the next five years it was the subject of eight divisions in Council debates. The main achievement of increased Tory representation was a vote in June 1841 to abandon the Armley project. The Liberals narrowly won the 1841 elections and in the 1840s regained a large Council majority, so Armley was once more restored and was finally opened in 1847. Municipal elections, open debates, corporate accounts, a police force, a prestigious gaol and of course daily justice from the borough magistrates, these were the harvest of 1835.

There were, however, a few indications that a handful of

people glimpsed a more positive municipal future. Baines, in the *Mercury*, argued that the regulation of house building ought to be a municipal function and warned against short sighted parsimony:

> In a large and increasing borough like ours neglected as it has been in some of its most important interests, viz. the cleanliness and good order of the town and the education of its poor inhabitants, expenses will have to be incurred which cannot be prevented.[11]

George Goodman, the first reform mayor, looked to the Council to 'effect a material improvement in the condition of the burgesses and identify themselves with the people to promote those objects which would tend to their happiness and prosperity.' It was Robert Baker, a doctor with experience in factory regulation and Poor Law administration, who articulated most clearly the need for a positive role for the Council. Baker, the butt of critics for his work in police reform as first chairman of the watch committee, persuaded the Council in 1838 to finance a statistical enquiry he organized to look into social conditions in Leeds township. His report provides valuable evidence on wage rates, occupational structure, crime, religion, education and the physical environment. (Baker, 1839.) When introducing the report to the Council in 1839, Baker stressed that physical conditions created nuisances which were prejudicial to health but which were avoidable. In demonstrating the relationship between environment and disease Baker had mapped out a potential area of municipal usefulness and he urged the Council to accept responsibility for the health and welfare of the urban populace:

> They were the representatives of the people and it was the legitimate object of all Corporations to look at those whom they represented in all their relations of life and he trusted that the time was not far distant when . . . both sides of the Council would take up this great question — a great public question he would call it — and never allow it to rest until all the improvements had been effected. . . . He would ask any one whether the moral and social condition of the poor in this town was not a matter of vital im-

portance . . . the working classes did look for an amelioration of their condition and they would ask it as a boon at the hands of the Council. . . . He called upon the Council as they valued their characters as Christians and philanthropists to extend the hand of sympathy and benevolence to those whom providence had not blessed with the same enjoyment as themselves.[12]

The Council as guardian of the moral and social conditon of the poor was a municipal role which was not to be fully publicized until the Birmingham 'civic gospel' thirty years later.

Baker found locally, as Chadwick did nationally shortly afterwards, that the confirmation of the environmental origin of high morbidity and mortality rates did not produce any immediate dividends. Despite Baker's eloquence, municipal 'economists' argued that nothing could be done about the nuisances complained of, and it was outside the Council that the first signs of movement on this question were to be detected. Even after 1835, it was the Improvement Commission and not the Council which was the main agent of urban amenity and the first effects of Baker's campaign were to be found in the commissioners' plans to seek a new and enlarged improvement act. Concern over public health prompted support for national legislation but when Whig proposals were published local reformers preferred to keep control firmly in local hands. Fear of centralization meant that Baker's work would flower in a local rather than a national context.

Even in local affairs there was an important constitutional issue to resolve concerning the location of the powers under the improvement bill launched in 1841. There were three possibilities. First, the Improvement Commission, the traditional authority in the field, might inherit the new powers and acquire new functions. Second, the tri-partite sponsoring committee for the bill, commissioners, councillors and magistrates, might continue thus drawing on a wide cross section of local leaders. Third, the Council might take over improvement functions on the ground that municipal reform had removed the impediments which had rendered the old Corporation unsuitable for these functions. The Council itself strongly supported this option.

Local political developments gave this question added significance, since Leeds Chartists, seeking to establish a political role for working men, had captured the Improvement Commission in January 1842. They set about amending the improvement bill in order to democratize local government. They were insistent that popular participation and control should be maintained and fashioned the clauses of the bill to achieve this. Powers were to be vested in the commissioners alone, with no role for bench or Council. Ratepayers were to elect commissioners who would have to satisfy only a residential but not a financial qualification. No projected expenditure over £500 would be allowed without the direct consent of ratepayers, and meetings to seek that consent were to be held in the evening. Rates were to be levied on a progressive scale by which houses under £10 were assessed at one third the rate of houses over £50. It was Chartism in practice in the search for popular democracy in local government.

This was strong medicine for the property owners who were backing the bill financially. The Council announced that it could not support the bill in view of the changes made, and they were closely followed by the magistrates. Even the legal representatives of the commissioners withdrew and the Chartists were forced to acknowledge with reluctance that without legal, financial and political support the bill would lapse. They therefore abandoned the bill in favour of national proposals but before so doing persuaded the vestry to resolve that no local bill was acceptable which did not contain the agreed democratic arrangements. This, the Chartist leader asserted, would prevent any section from using 'their party political and legislatorial influence to procure the passing of the Bill in a shape to suit their own party and class interests but in a shape objectionable to the majority of the inhabitants.' Despite this ban the bill was resuscitated, the offending democratic clauses amended and the proposals put to Parliament for a decision. The Leeds Improvement Act of 1842 vested all powers in the Town Council, with which the Improvement Commission was merged. The creation and amalgamation of powers meant that in many ways 1842 was a more important watershed in Leeds local government history than was 1835.

The 1842 Act was wide ranging in its provisions, and it elevated the Council from a political and legal institution to a social and sanitary authority. It contained 392 clauses, empowering the Council to pave, light and cleanse the streets, to construct a system of sewerage and drainage, to impose building regulations for both internal and external features of houses, to supervise markets and hackney carriages, to build a town hall, to acquire property for improvement, if necessary by compulsory purchase, and to control smoke pollution. It authorized the Council to levy three rates (a general rate for sewerage, an improvement rate for specific schemes and a lamp rate for lighting) and to borrow £100,000. The Council set up nine separate committees to administer the Act. It created a precedent, which Manchester, Liverpool and Birmingham were soon to follow, for large towns to advance the cause of public health reform through private local acts rather than general national ones. Nevertheless a number of the clauses in the 'untrodden fields' of sewerage and building regulation were taken directly from the abortive Whig bills of 1841 (Barber, 1975, 59–72).

It was with Robert Baker that the new Act was mainly identified, and it was he who explained its provisions and implications to the Council. It was therefore Baker who was held personally responsible for the increased expenditure consequent on the Act. Within a few months angry protest meetings were held in Baker's ward which called on him to resign. Baker's constituents made their position clear:

> Do they not all suffer from the injuries that your public extravagance may inflict? . . . Are they not all called upon to pay their proportion of the cost of your expensive schemes and speculations?[13]

In the spring of 1843 many wards had similar 'economist' meetings and Baker did not return to the Council when his term expired in November. The new popular hero was a tea merchant who had been prominent twenty years earlier in demands for retrenchment in parochial expenditure. Now he set the tone of the moment by proclaiming, 'the people were more solicitous about draining rates from their pockets than draining the streets.' Where historians see great benefits many contemporaries saw only huge costs.

Cries for economy were symptomatic of public nervousness about both costs and powers involved in the extension of municipal government and the outcry recurred after later enlargement of corporate functions. They also owed something to the general economic climate; as Leeds emerged from the early Victorian depression so a more expansive mood prevailed. By 1845 that same Chartist leader who had democratized the 1842 improvement bill, Joshua Hobson, now a Councillor, was advocating the purchase and demolition of insanitary property to lay out a wide new street of shops. The dozen years from the passage of the Improvement Act were characterized, despite the economists, by extensive municipal activity in public health reform, particularly in the areas of sewerage and of water supply.

The creation of a main drainage and sewerage system for the whole borough proved a more protracted process than had been anticipated, and it was not until 1850 that work began, and not until 1855 that the scheme was completed. The Council had begun in 1843 by draining an unsanitary area in the eastern part of Leeds township and had then embarked on the preparatory work for the design of a sewerage system for the rest of the borough. This was no easy task, for there were severe technical difficulties associated with the low lying areas south of the river Aire. There were four separate reports commissioned by the Council, whose members might certainly have quoted the nineteenth century saying 'what can the layman do when the doctors disagree?'. The doctors, in this case surveyors and civil engineers, provided conflicting advice between 1844 and 1848 on which councillors, without professional expertise, found it difficult to adjudicate. Moreover, progress was frustrated by legal disputes with members of several vested interests over water rights and benefits, real or imagined, to be derived from the sale of sewage as agricultural manure. The financial limits of the 1842 Act and some uncertainty over powers convinced the

Council that new legislation was required and so the Council spent £3,000 and more time in securing an appropriate Act in 1848. Yet by the beginning of 1849, when the scheme was ready to be launched, the whole economic climate had changed and economic depression revived fears of expense. The change was evidenced by the contrasting positions adopted by William Brook, a leading Chartist Councillor. In 1846-7 Brook complained bitterly of the delay in implementing the sewerage scheme because of middle-class indifference to working-class sickness. The working class, he reported, favoured the sewerage project because 'they dread the doctor's bill more than the rate.' By 1849 unemployment and low wages had made it impossible for his constituents to pay their inflated poor rates, and so Brook advocated delay, now asserting that 'want of food more than want of sewerage was the great creator of disease.'

Ironically it was disease itself that finally overwhelmed 'economist' opposition. In January and February 1849 the Council had voted not to proceed with the sewerage scheme it had taken six years to mature. The second visitation of cholera, which claimed 2,000 lives in the summer of 1849, gave sewerage a novel priority. Contemporaries referred to the 'Boon of Cholera' which had transformed opinion and which had instructed 'cashiered town councillors that they were false to their functions and clumsy speculators for popularity when instead of checking they encouraged the short sighted and mistaken economy of ratepayers.'[14] Because of concern over cholera the Leeds Council in September 1849 reversed its earlier decision and agreed to go ahead, a decision confirmed in November by the vote of a fourpenny rate to finance the scheme. The sewerage system was completed in 1855, and as usual the estimate of £80,000 was exceeded by the actual cost of £137,000. Between 1850 and 1862 the Council spent over £211,000 on the main sewerage system.

An even greater sum was involved in the municipal water supply. When this question had first been discussed in the 1830s, technical, ideological and political issues were raised, causing great controversy (Thoresby, 1970). The Leeds Waterworks Act of 1837 had authorized a partnership between

Council and the shareholders who jointly managed the town's water supply. In the late 1840s full municipal ownership became a distinct possibility. In 1848 and 1850 Edwin Eddison, a former town clerk and now a Liberal Councillor, suggested that the Council should purchase water and gas companies. Some change in water policy was inevitable, for the company had been unable to discover new sources of supply to meet the growing demand for water. Some who opposed public monopolies argued that increased competition, and not corporate control, was the answer:

> The pecuniary success of waterworks will depend chiefly like any other enterprise on ability and vigilance in management and all experience goes to prove that these conditions are best secured by the direct interest of those who undertake them. . . . The burgesses may rest assured that whatever else be the result an increased amount of local taxation will accrue from our municipal water cure.[15]

Such doubts were brushed aside by a Liberal solicitor, Alderman John Hope Shaw, whose able advocacy convinced the Council that it should take over this social utility. His case rested on a simple rhetorical question that demonstrated his view of the proper role of the Council — 'was it not the duty of the municipal body to look to the welfare of the people they represented?' Public evidence confirmed the shortage of water and medical testimony indicated its harmful effects on health. If the Leeds community needed water, the Leeds Town Council could not stand idly by. In the summer of 1851 Hope Shaw's reports carried the day, and when his scheme came up for confirmation in April 1852 he asserted 'the Town Council was the proper body to manage the supply of water and no principle of trade would be violated by their undertaking the management of such works.' The Corporation purchase of the Leeds Waterworks Company was completed in November 1852 at a cost of over £227,000. As 'economists' witnessed this addition to the municipal debt they ruefully observed that not one extra drop of water had been thereby provided. Hope Shaw advised that the river Washburn was the best available source, but the Council, partly for financial reasons, accepted a scheme for a pumping station from the Wharfe, despite the risk of pollution. The 1856 Leeds Waterworks Act authorized the new works, which were to provide 2·5m gallons per day, but which were to prove of only short term benefit.

Sewerage and water supply were but the main planks in a municipal sanitary programme that also included new burial grounds, household refuse collection, the purchase of Woodhouse Moor and the appointment of inspectors for smoke pollution and slaughterhouses. In enlarging Kirkgate Market the Council had cleared the most notorious health hazard in the town, the Boot and Shoe Yard, though it was its proximity to the market site rather than its sanitary reputation that caused its demolition. Corporate activity ranged from the removal of bridge tolls to the management of the newly built Armley Gaol. In the 1850s the building of the Town Hall symbolized the enlarged horizons of municipal administration in Leeds. The Town Hall project was controversial from the outset and it was prone to political, economic and contractual difficulties. In the end the 'magnificent' triumphed over the 'meagre' and the Town Hall, 'an outward symbol of public government,' was completed with the embellishment of its ornamental tower. It was indeed an example of civic pride (Briggs, 1963, 138–83). And when Queen Victoria, officially opening the Town Hall in 1858, granted the mayor, Peter Fairbairn, a knighthood it was an accolade for the whole concept of municipal government in Leeds.

The Town Hall was the most important symbol of mid-Victorian municipal administration in Leeds, and its very completion was a yardstick of Council achievement. Yet there was another more fundamental measure of the Council's first quarter century. The 'great fact' of municipal life was the death rate. If the key to the growth of municipal administration was concern for public health then corporate success would be registered in a falling death rate. As Chadwick had demonstrated, a high proportion of urban deaths were from 'avoidable' diseases. In Leeds, as in Liverpool, a falling and hence comforting trend in death rates in the later 1850s was reversed in the 1860s. Death rates of well over 30 per thousand in the 1840s had been reduced to about

27 per thousand in the late 1850s but in the 1860s the figure approached 30 once more. Indeed in the first quarter of 1865 a death rate of 32·3 per thousand was recorded, which was substantially higher than the average urban death rate in England as a whole. It was widely believed that 'the excessive mortality in Leeds is, to a great extent, within its own control' and it was of course the Town Council who were primarily responsible for exercising that control (Braithwaite, 1865, 5). That it had demonstrably failed to arrest the growth in 'excessive mortality' was thus a major criticism of the Council. There were also more positive results of maladministration. The Council was itself summoned for maintaining a nuisance prejudicial to health in the matter of the soil heap at its refuse collection centre. Moreover, the town's high death rate in 1865 prompted a medical inspection by a Privy Council inspector who lashed the Corporation with stinging criticism. Dr. Hunter found Leeds 'a surprising sight, bringing to remembrance the condition of many English towns of twenty years ago,' and his superior Sir John Simon, parrying the chauvinistically hostile Leeds response, reported in 1866 that Leeds health administration 'in proportion to the importance of the town may perhaps be deemed the worst which has ever come to the knowledge of this department' (Lambert, 1963, 434).

REACTION AND ECONOMY

How had Leeds Town Council come to draw such criticism when it had pioneered local legislation for environmental control? Much of the answer lay in the intermittent nature of municipal energy and enthusiasm, and the consequently erratic exercise of municipal functions. Historians have found that municipal involvement was liable to fluctuate between peaks of activity and troughs of inertia. The problems were always so complex, the routine administration so tedious and the results so minimal that municipal enthusiasm was invariably dulled by the passage of time. In municipal affairs the evils were always so much more deeply rooted and the anticipated gains so much more elusive than had been expected. So in Leeds powers were patchily exercised. The compulsory purchase powers in the 1842 Act were largely unutilized because the process was found to be so costly when first attempted, since arbitration juries always favoured the private property owner in valuations. The planning regulations had not been fully enforced and many nuisance prosecutions were abandoned because of doubts over legal powers. By the mid-1860s both the water supply and the sewerage scheme were in need of extension, and the value of the latter had always been weakened by the failure to compel the connection of house drains into the main sewers. Probably most important of all, the Council had failed to provide itself with a sufficient inspectorate for the enforcement of health regultions.

This fluctuating commitment to environmental control itself reflected the changing social composition of the Council. Though Chartists complained in the early 1840s that wealthy Councillors were indifferent to the sanitary needs of the working class, it was in fact the upper working-class and lower middle-class elected representatives who were most hostile to sanitary expenditure. As more shopkeepers, tradesmen, small merchants, artisans, craftsmen and publicans came into the Council so municipal energy waned. It was such Councillors whom the housing reformer James Hole (Harrison, 1954) had in mind when he wrote scathingly in 1866:

> They and those who elect them are the lower middle class, the owners generally speaking of that very property which requires improvement. To ask them to close the cellar dwellings is to ask them to forfeit a portion of their incomes. Every pound they vote for drainage or other sanitary improvement is something taken out of their own pocket . . . to the ratepayers themselves a little claptrap about centralisation and still more an appeal to their pockets . . . is sufficient to cause the rejection of the most useful measure.[16]

Beyond the councillors lay a volatile electorate aware of the financial implications of sanitary reform, and we should not forget that councillors had to seek re-election every three years. The annual municipal elections were the Victorian equivalent of our opinion polls, sensitive indicators of local public opinion. Though strident 'economist' pressure was not a feature of the early 1860s (itself evidence of reduced Council activity) the mayor could nevertheless assert in 1865 that 'municipal economy' was the main cause of Council inertia:

> If public opinion had supported the council, they would not now have had only one Inspector, but three or four inspectors of nuisances . . . they needed a public opinion to back them, for so long as the public were crying out, 'economy, economy' and upbraiding the council for spending money on what they deemed most advantageous, they made the council what they were . . . the great difficulty with which they had to contend was this constant cry for economy.[17]

That same public who cried out for economy were ambivalent and could soon adopt a quite different posture. As always, support for municipal expenditure varied directly with the death rate, and the high death rates of the mid-1860s had produced acute public concern well before the Medical Department of the Privy Council administered its sharp reprimand. Indeed, in raising the hackles of the Council, Simon and Hunter may have delayed further sanitary improvement in Leeds, because the path of reform was temporarily diverted into local patriotism. The Council felt obliged to defend the town against an unwarranted official attack before rooting out the evils which provoked it. The Privy Council was stridently informed 'we are not ashamed of our town, nor afraid to live in it.' However, when the honour of Leeds had been defended the Council did return to the sanitary problems which contributed to the high death rates, even if they had been exaggerated by statistical distortions. The question came back to one of powers. What was true of national social policy in early and mid-Victorian Britain was equally true of local sanitary policy. It was only by operating the legislation that its deficiencies could be exposed and the problems fully explored. Initial legislation bred the need for further legislation. By 1865–6 the vital need for a new and more extensive improvement bill was recognized.

The lack of real power, together with a lack of public confidence in the effectiveness or legality of existing power, had severely constrained municipal administration in mid-Victorian Leeds. It was this, rather than 'municipal economy,' which a prominent sanitary reformer Frederick Baines cited in February 1865. The *Leeds Mercury*, which Frederick Baines now edited, had been actively campaigning for sanitary reform and at an important public meeting Baines explained the limits on the Council:

> there was no power to compel the owners of property to sewer land before building human habitations on it . . . they had no power to prevent back to back houses, no power to require any street however long to exceed 30 feet in width nor to bear any fitting relation to existing streets and no power to compel the sewering and paving of the multitudinous new streets not thoroughfares . . . there was no power to forbid cellar dwellings. . . . The Council had not the power to prevent the erection of new *culs de sac*, those stoppings of fresh air of which they had so long been complaining . . . the Council had no power whatever to compel the owners of old property to connect their dwelling houses with the drains.[18]

The need for new powers was thus clearly expounded and to some that need was manifest in the very physical appearance of the town. As James Hole pointedly explained, radicals normally pressed for greater individual liberty, but

> when contemplating an ugly ill built town, where every little freeholder asserts his indefensible rights as a Briton to do what he likes with his own; to inflict his own selfishness, ignorance and obstinacy upon his neighbours or posterity for generations to come and where local *self*-government means merely misgovernment — we are apt to wish for a little wholesome despotism to curb such vagaries.[19]

The 'wholesome despotism' came in the form of the 1866 Improvement Act, which extended the Council's powers and its borrowing rights. At last Leeds followed the example of Liverpool and gained the powers to appoint a Medical Officer of Health whose authority would make nuisance removal procedures more effective. The first M.O.H., Dr. M. K. Robinson, was able to add medical weight to the campaign for continued sanitary improvement in the town. The 1866 Act also merged the powers of the highway surveyors in the Council and so yet another local government rival succumbed to corporate control. A fragmented system was becoming increasingly unified under municipal authority. The Council, which previously had some street responsibilities, was now in a position to enforce a uniform roads policy throughout the borough.

MUNICIPAL REVIVAL

The 1866 Improvement Act inaugurated a period of wide ranging Council activity. Under its powers two major street improvements were set in motion. The Boar Lane scheme particularly aroused great public interest and enthusiasm: there were two rival proposals, one for a straight street, the other for a crooked one; in the 1866 elections the war cry was 'rush to the polls and vote for the straight street and down with all doglegs.' So great was public enthusiasm that the Council was pushed into a more ambitious scheme than originally planned. In the aftermath of this largesse yet another Act in 1869 endowed the Council with powers to acquire much larger sites for redevelopment. The 1866 Act enabled the Council to purchase road and bridge tolls, and in the next three years £66,000 was spent on freeing roads and bridges. In 1866 and 1869 the Council obtained special powers to clear up the foetid streams which ran into the Aire, and by 1869 a major scheme of sewerage extension was also approved, which grouped the out-townships of the borough into a single drainage district. In 1867 the Council established a refuse removal department and shortly afterwards a legal dispute over sewage disposal pushed the Council towards the system of sewage utilization finally adopted in 1877. Though the Council had no power to ban back to backs it adopted a by-law in 1866 limiting such developments to blocks of eight houses with a controlled amount of air around them. Perhaps the most ambitious Council programme was the enlargement of the water supply under the 1867 Leeds Waterworks Act. The limits of the Wharfe supply were now generally accepted, and the great

Washburn scheme was adopted with its three reservoirs (Lindley Wood 1875, Swinsty 1876, Fewston 1879).

Such a catalogue of municipal endeavour found its natural echo in increased rates, which in turn revived ratepayers' 'economist' fears. G. A. Linsley, a pawnbroker and Councillor led the attack by arguing,

> The desire for public improvement is becoming almost a mania and I regret to say that it is well represented in the Council. Do these gentlemen ever think about the increasing taxation and obligations of the borough and that over taxation tends to injury? I fear not.[20]

He helped to found the Leeds Municipal Reform Association in 1868 which was pledged to municipal economy, and in the 1869 elections there was a victory for what Linsley termed economy over expenditure with the defeat of two retiring Councillors in West Ward. When the mayor came to be elected his main attraction was his support for retrenchment, for as one of his supporters noticed, 'by the recent elections the ratepayers had shown that they were extremely anxious to put the drag on and stop the extravagance of the Council.' The origin of this public uneasiness was clear for all to see in the growth of the borough debt and increased rates, especially as a consequence of the 1866 Act. Both are indicated in Tables 3.2 and 3.3.

Table 3.2   *Borough Debt, Leeds Corporation 1842–1867*

	Water- works	Town hall	Gaol	Im- prove- ment	Sewer	Total
1842				15,700		15,700
1847			33,760	52,400		86,160
1852	227,100	9,430	32,260	46,400	57,580	373,040
1857	275,786	55,512	24,000	75,570	100,040	530,908
1862	308,906	88,524	16,500	98,923	97,722	610,575
1866	344,489	98,972	11,500	122,644	101,705	676,410
1867	347,686	99,500	6,500	238,275	109,189	801,150

Table 3.3   Borough Rates, Leeds Corporation
1842–1867

	High-way	Sewer	Lamp	Im-prove-ment	Gaol	Borough/Watch	Total
1842			6d.	7d.	1½d.	1s. 0¼d.	2s. 2¾d.
1847			6d.	7d.	1½d.	1s. 0¾d.	2s. 3¼d.
1852		4d.	6d.	7d.	1½d.	10½d.	2s. 5d.
1857		8d.	5d.	7d.	1½d.	1s. 0d.	2s. 9½d.
1862		8d.	4d.	10d.	1½d.	1s. 1½d.	3s. 1d.
1866		8d.	5d.	1s. 0d.	1½d.	1s. 1d.	3s. 3¼d.
1867	1s. 6d.	8d.	5d.	1s. 0d.	1½d.	1s. 2d.	4s. 10½d.

A borough debt of £800,000 produced its corollary in a borough rate of 4s. 10½d. in the pound in 1867. The latter was exaggerated by the highway rate levied for the first time by the Council in 1867. The Highway Surveyors in each township had previously levied this rate, which had never exceeded 10d, yet the first time the Council acted as surveyors it was raised to 1s. 6d. There were two reasons for this. First, the out-townships had always maintained roads at a minimum level which depressed the rate below its real need. Because it was agreed to have a uniform rate throughout the borough, previous suburban parsimony now produced a large rise across the board. The second reason for the sharp increase was that the expectation of Council amalgamation had induced surveyors to depress the rates even more than usual, leaving the Council with much remedial maintenance to deal with.

Such increased rate demands produced accusations that the Council was intrinsically a more expensive public body than the township organs it replaced and this fuelled the economist campaign. Furthermore, this and the prospect of another £400,000 to be spent on the water supply caused many to question whether corporate functions had not proceeded much too far. An angry ratepayer gleefully cited one of the Council's own professional advisers in support of the proposition that Councils were unfit to control the social environment:

Almost the entire of their attention is devoted to objects of a political, party or personal nature . . . involved in continuous rancorous contests they have neither the time the inclination nor the ability to devote themselves dispassionately to the subject of local improvement. . . . I feel impressed with the importance of withholding the power of becoming traders in or distributors of public necessity or public utility from the hands of a body so incompetent, so ill informed and so unstable as Municipal Corporations.[21]

Yet neither such fundamental doubts nor the 'pocket argument' could effectively delay the march of the municipal leviathan in Leeds. In the nature of the case the ratepayers' resistance focused on symbolic small issues, especially corporate salaries, rather than on large schemes of expenditure, which moved almost under the weight of their own momentum. Corporation salaries were a key political issue in 1870 but this did not prevent the 1870 Leeds Improvement and Gas Act from passing and under this Act the Council purchased the two gas companies at a cost of three quarters of a million pounds. The economists could save hundreds on salaries while the Council spent thousands. In the short term the high valuation of the works together with increased coal prices (which under the terms of the Act could not be recouped from consumers) meant that the Council had to subsidize the gas concern rather than the other way round. However in the first decade of working, gas profits of £40,000 were accumulated for the corporate account. A similar large scale project which was immune to the economists' resistance was the 1871 purchase of Roundhay Park for £139,000. This was a prestige project which, because of distance and lack of transport, was of limited popular value until the tramways of the 1890s. The immediate significance was that both the gas and park purchases were approved while the economists were in full cry.

As always public opinion was double-edged. The ratepayers' movement had scored an impressive victory in West Ward in 1869, and two economists were returned in Hunslet and Holbeck in 1870, yet the new popular hero of retrenchment, the fruit merchant Archie Scarr, was defeated in West Ward in 1870 and 1871. Scarr was able to enter the Council only when he stood as a Liberal in North East Ward in 1872. Sanitary reformers were not as noisy as economists but they were as constant to their cause. When the M.O.H., acting under the 1870 Act, condemned property off Kirkgate in 1871 which was notoriously insanitary this action was loudly applauded, and the *Mercury* commented 'the public health is more important than vested interests'. A large and very influential deputation from the Social Improvement Society addressed the Council in 1874 in order

> to urge upon the Council increased attention to the sanitary condition of the borough. The prevalent evils arising from crowded, ill drained and ill ventilated dwellings in poor districts were forcibly described . . . The high death rate was urged as the result of neglect of sanitary laws and a powerful appeal was made in the interest of the poor for more strict supervision over and action in dealing with several remediable evils.[22]

As ever, sanitary reform needed sustained vigilance as well as enforcement of regulations, and at the time of this deputation the death rate was nearly 29 per thousand. It dropped below 25 after 1876 but did not fall consistently below 20 until the very end of the century. In removing by clearance order those nearest to the source of disease the Council found that in the absence of alternative housing provision the very poor simply crowded into other unsanitary property. It was the gradual recognition of this problem which led the Council to include in its 1877 Improvement Act a clause empowering the Corporation to acquire land for working-class housing and to build and let the houses as a municipal function.

Such powers were pioneering but not immediately operated, and the 1877 Act marked the end of a hectic phase of Leeds municipal history. Partly because of a changed atmosphere created by an economist public opinion, partly because the Council was controlled by petty bourgeois and artisan councillors and partly because it simply ran out of steam, the decade of municipal zeal that ended in 1877 was followed by another period of inertia. The municipal ebb and flow was once more triggered off by sanitary concern, following a typhoid epidemic in 1889. During this 'new era' of municipal reform sanitary improvement was given a cutting edge by fierce party political rivalry which after sixty years finally gave the Conservatives control of the Leeds Council (Hennock, 1973, 257). The 1890s were characterized by slum slearance on a large scale, more rigorous enforcement of sanitary regulations through the energetic M.O.H. Dr. J. S. Cameron, the public purchase of the privately owned tramways and electric lighting companies, the provision of swimming baths and public works schemes for the relief of the unemployed. By the early twentieth century Leeds Corporation employed nearly 4,000, serving the public in nine separate departments. This was perhaps some indication of the extent to which the Council had fulfilled the first reform mayor's hope that it would 'effect a material improvement in the condition of the burgesses and promote those objects which would tend to their happiness and prosperity.'

Four
Birmingham

MUNICIPAL REFORM AND INCORPORATION

The rapid growth of Birmingham in the late eighteenth century was a remarkable feature of the Industrial Revolution. According to one estimate, its population more than doubled in the last three decades of the century as its range of hardware trades multiplied. Highly skilled metal workers, flexible enough to turn their hands to many tasks, gave Birmingham a primacy in meeting the needs of the new industrial society. Birmingham could supply anything from steam engines to steel pens. Its social structure bred harmony between classes, its economic character protected it from the worst of trade depressions and its physical location provided not only natural business advantages but also a healthy climate. In time elements of class war, economic slump and the insanitary environment became local issues of importance, but in each case the problems were less serious than in many other growing cities.

Birmingham's rapid development occurred without the aid of a corporation, for unlike Leeds and Liverpool the town was unincorporated. It was governed by its traditional manorial and parochial institutions as though it were still a small village. Yet this was never seen as a disadvantage. Indeed the freedom from corporate regulation was cited as one of the main reasons why the town had flourished. Migrants from Britain and overseas, many of them religious and political refugees, were able to settle freely, for Birmingham was 'a town without shackle' (Hutton, 1795). A directory of 1805 recorded that its lack of a corporation 'not a little contributes to increase its trade, buildings and inhabitants' while a guide of 1818 explained that because Birmingham had no charter 'strangers from whatever quarter they may come here find an asylum and pursue their avocations.'[1] By mid-century, when Langford produced his great compilation on the history of Birmingham, this theme had become conventional local wisdom:

> Birmingham was a free town. No guild or corporation imposed restriction upon citizenship; and so the industrious, the ingenious and the perserving found this their natural home where each could develop his facilities unfettered.[2]

No doubt the significance of this urban freedom was exaggerated, and in any case the ever-increasing problems associated with rapid growth soon made a disadvantage out of a supposed advantage. A town that had already exceeded 100,000 in population by 1821 could not forever enjoy unregulated freedom; attempts were made during the 1820s to impose greater order upon Birmingham affairs. These mainly comprised efforts to strengthen the three skeletal local government agencies, the manorial, parochial and improvement institutions (Stephens, 1964). Manorial authority, such as it was, devolved upon the Court Leet whose jury annually elected the High and Low Bailiffs together with a variety of quaint officials such as Headborough and Ale Conners. There had been attempts in the eighteenth century to pack the juries of the Court Leet, so the manorial system must have had some local importance, but functionally it was effete. It was the ineffectiveness of Manchester's manorial institutions that convinced Cobden of the need for incorporation, yet the Manchester bodies were far more active than those in Birmingham. Nevertheless, the offices of High and Low Bailiff did acquire some status and, since the former was normally a leading Anglican and the latter a leading Dissenter, the posts came to personify the symbolic authority of social leadership in the town. In the absence of a mayor the High Bailiff became his surrogate, gradually by custom and convention exercising the functions of urban authority. This process was arrested by political divisions in the emerging elite, since implicit unofficial power could not be exercised without the common consent of those unofficially ruled. When in 1821 a group of Tories objected to the manner in which the Liberal High Bailiff G. F. Muntz, later M.P. for Birmingham, had demonstrated his political bias, they passed a resolution which called a halt to a well established trend:

> The High Bailiff has of right no authority within the town, except as the bailiff of the lord of the manor, appointed to proclaim the fairs, to superintend and preserve good order therein, and in the markets, and to regulate the weights measures throughout the town. His presence does not necessarily give a sanction to any public meeting; the importance which has for a few years attached to the office of High Bailiff has been a matter of courtesy only.[3]

When on the celebrated occasion in January 1830 the then Tory High Bailiff refused to call a public meeting to launch Attwood's Birmingham Political Union, it was merely a confirmation that political conflict had irreversibly consigned the town's leading honorific post to a merely manorial role.*

The parochial institutions were perhaps more favourably placed on which to graft quasi-municipal functions. In 1783 the parish of Birmingham had adopted Gilbert's Act and set up a Board of Guardians for the administration of the Poor Law. This body was elected by ratepayers and comprised the 'wealth and respectability' of the town. In the later 1820s the guardians planned a new act which would have enlarged their functions beyond mere poor relief. In 1828–9 a bill was drawn up to empower the guardians to light, watch, drain, cleanse and pave the streets, to introduce by-laws and even to raise a loan for the building of a town hall. In effect the Board of Guardians wished to transform itself into an embryonic municipal council. Much controversy surrounded this proposal again for political reasons. The faction controlling the Board, nicknamed 'the Cabal,' had sought to perpetuate its power by devious means. For instance, in 1828 the twelve overseers had produced a secret list of nominations for guardians in order to by-pass the popular election. Because of

---

*The High Bailiff's decision was applauded by the anti-Attwood *Aris's Birmingham Gazette*, 18 Jan., 1830, and criticized by the pro-Attwood *Birmingham Journal*, 23 Jan., 1830, thus demonstrating that the High Bailiff could speak for only part of the town.

this many were deeply suspicious of entrusting enlarged powers to such a body. With obvious glee, one observer recorded the defeat of the Cabal through the loss of this bill and commented, 'their attempt to introduce *borough rule* and *corporation doings* into Birmingham has been met as it ought and treated as it deserved.'[4] When the new local Act was finally obtained in 1831 it provided for new rating powers as planned in the earlier draft but the 'Borough rule' and 'corporation doings' were discarded.

In fact the body which assumed the largest local government functions was the Street Commission, first appointed under a local Act of 1769. The Street Commission obtained five Improvement Acts between 1769 and 1828 which progressively enlarged its functions and increased its powers. This in itself is not so surprising for we have already seen that in Leeds and Liverpool it was the Improvement Commission and not the Corporation which was responsible for any serious environmental control. Yet there was a striking difference between the Birmingham Street Commission and analogous improvement institutions elsewhere. In corporate towns the improvement commissions were often elected by the ratepayers in vestry and acted as an open political institution in contrast to the closed self-elected corporations. But in Birmingham there was no corporation and the Street Commission became a substitute corporation with a close self-elective constitution. Hence the open vestry was a rival not to an oligarchic corporation but to an oligarchic improvement commission. No doubt when the Street Commission was first established it was still fashionable to create self-elected commissions but by the 1820s the process of renewal by co-option was widely criticized. Despite this the 1828 Act preserved the oligarchic nature of the commission while endowing it with new powers, including the right to build a new town hall.

There were two reasons why the Street Commission was able to deflect public criticism and retain its self-elective character until its demise in 1851. The first concerned recruitment of the elite. In the final analysis it was the political exclusiveness of the unreformed corporations which caused their downfall, because they alienated their political opponents. The Birmingham Street Commission, however, studiously avoided politics, and was able to operate as the natural focus of authority in the town by recruiting across a wide range of opinions. In particular it was able to smother protest movements by co-opting potential opponents. This was seen clearly in the background to the 1828 Act, which had been first mooted in 1825. In view of likely resistance the commissioners had agreed to delay the proposed bill until they had negotiated with a committee of ratepayers which included Joseph Parkes. By 1828 a number of leading critics had been successfully bought off by co-option on to the Commission and it was noticed what a remarkable change occurred in radical opinion:

> It is scarcely possible to conceive a more strict oligarchy than that of the Commissioners of the Birmingham Street Acts, yet so great are the illuminations which the former democratic party of this town lately received that such a constitution now seems — so long as they form a part thereof — the very *beau ideal* of good government . . . the former friends of universal suffrage not only now deprecate the idea of ratepayers appointing the persons by whom their money is to be expended but actually connive at the practice of keeping the people wholly in the dark as to the manner in which the money is laid out.[5]

A successful recruitment policy was allied secondly to efficient administration. Again the contrast with the corporations was significant. Birmingham was well governed by the Street Commission and ultimately it was the Commission's record of growing environmental activity which was its best defence. (Gill, 1952, Chap. IX.) As one of its supporters explained in relation to the 1828 Act, 'the plans are the result of close and long continued attention to the subject and are essentially calculated to advance the comfort and convenience of the inhabitants and materially to improve the general appearance and character of the town.'[6] It was under the powers of the 1828 Act that Birmingham Town Hall was built, still standing as a monument to the regime not of a corporation but of the Street Commission.

The Commission, though a quasi-corporation, was naturally immune from the effects of the 1835 Municipal Corporations Act, and Birmingham, like other unincorporated towns, was not immediately touched by it. Yet Birmingham radical opinion shared the political ideals of reformers in corporate towns where the nature of municipal government was widely applauded. In the early years of municipal reform radicals looked not to the administrative role of the councils but to their political constitution for the main advantage of reformed over unreformed local government. Open representative government was the great virtue of the new system and it was the lack of it in Birmingham which mattered most. The Street Commission administered its functions efficiently but that did not compensate in radical eyes for the denial of the essential principles of local government as they were now manifest in corporate towns. As an ardent reformer put it:

> We have our Court Leet and our Bailiffs, chosen by themselves; our Town Hall Commissioners, chosen by themselves; working in the dark, unseen by the public eye, irresponsible to the public voice, appointing their own officers, levying taxes at their pleasure and distributing them, without check or control, as their inclination shall determine.[7]

It was the political ideology of municipal reform which informed the incorporation movement of 1837.

In Birmingham, as in Manchester at the same time (and in Bradford and Salford in the next decade), incorporation produced a bitter polarization of political opinion. As Birmingham's first municipal historian explained, the fissures in town society ran very deep:

> So far was opposition carried that the town was literally split into social as well as political factions. Members of the two parties refused to meet in public or private, to engage in united action of any kind, to join in the same assemblies, or even to speak to each other in the streets. Each side attributed to the other the basest motives and the most dangerous designs; even business relations were not conducted without strain.[8]

Incorporation battles in all towns involved a conflict between new and traditional forms of government and a struggle for supremacy between rival elites within urban society. Birmingham was again different in one important respect. In many towns incorporation produced a Tory-radical alliance against middle-class Liberalism. Paternalistic traditional governors of the town joined with working-class radicals to resist bourgeois hegemony. Thus in Manchester, Tory anti-incorporation groups, entrenched in the parochial institutions, were given powerful aid by working-class radicals who feared what they termed 'the tyranny of the bloated rich.' It did appear that middle-class capitalists who already had a stranglehold on the town's economy were intent upon endowing their economic and social power with political authority. The Tory-radical alliance in Manchester was echoed in Bradford and Salford a decade later.

No such development occurred in Birmingham for two reasons. Firstly the social structure of the town bred social harmony rather than class conflict. It was the small workshop and not the factory which dominated the Birmingham economy, and masters and men were more closely bound together than, for instance, in some Lancashire cotton towns. Middle and working-class discontent moved in unison and found political expression in the class cooperation of Attwood's Birmingham Political Union (B.P.U.) (Briggs, 1948). At least until 1839 when Chartism undermined Attwood's position, the B.P.U. spoke for both working-class radicals and middle-class Liberals and so both groups supported incorporation. There was no focus for radical hostility, secondly, because of the role of the B.P.U. in local affairs. The significance of Attwood's organization in the passing of the 1832 Reform Act has rightly established the importance of the B.P.U. in the parliamentary reform movement. It is, however, often not fully appreciated that the B.P.U. was much more than a successful extra-parliamentary pressure group. From the outset Attwood aimed to create a body which would speak for the town by virtue of its role in local affairs. In particular it would oust the Cabal from its controlling position and it was resolved in January 1830 that 'the Union would . . . prevent and redress as far as practicable all the local public wrongs and oppressions and all local encroachments upon the rights, interests and privileges of the community.' Eighteen months later hardly any branch of town government had remained immune from B.P.U. influence. As the radical George Edmonds explained,

> Messrs Churchwardens, have you not found that you are responsible for your acts, and that you must yearly give a faithful account of your stewardship? Messrs Constables, have you discovered that you cannot commit wrong without being brought to the bar of public opinion? Messrs Governors of the Free Grammar School . . . have we not make you strike your flag and submit to the influence of popular opinion? Messrs Guardians of the Poor, has not the Political Union purged your body by the introduction of some of its members and enforced a principle of purity in your proceedings?[9]

There was thus a strong bridge between the B.P.U. in 1831 and the incorporation movement in 1837. In demanding incorporation the B.P.U. spoke for and not against working-class radicalism, so much so that the eventual Council was regarded by opponents as a 'legalised political union.'

It was Political Union radicals who originated the incorporation movement in March 1837 and they who organized the incorporation petition in November. Political issues dominated the incorporation campaign, which centred mainly on the principle of representation and the power of the new corporation. The familiar contrast was expounded between the closed self-elective traditional system and the impending new regime based upon democratic representation. As one reformer explained, 'society, the source of all power . . . should itself have the power of appointing its own officers and of conferring those social honours and distinctions, whatever they might be, which the necessities of society required.' The imminent corporation was expected above all to be a political institution, almost a new political fact in the government of the town and even the country. William Redfern, soon to be Birmingham's first Town Clerk, predicted that 'a new and gigantic power would be created — a power able in the case of need . . . to teach a lesson of humility to the House of Lords,' while Attwood in similar vein explained that 'they would possess a great political engine which would enable them to work the most important political purposes for their country.'[10] In November 1837 an incorporation petition signed by 4,000 inhabitants was sent to the Privy Council and an early grant of a charter was expected.

Yet there was to be a year's delay because of local opposition to incorporation. Four industrial towns, Manchester, Birmingham, Bolton and Sheffield, petitioned for a charter in 1837–8, and in all four towns a counter-petition was presented. Politics lay at the heart of it. It was feared that incorporation would remove power and status from traditional urban governors and extend powers to previously excluded groups, usually Liberal dissenters. In Birmingham, besides, even some Whigs opposed incorporation because they were themselves entrenched in the Street Commission, which as we noticed included leading citizens of all parties. The origin of the counter-petition in Birmingham lay in the truism that the B.P.U. did not speak for the whole town. The facts were simply recorded by a moderate Conservative newspaper. It wrote of the meeting which agreed to seek incorporation, 'none of the Conservative portion of our fellow townsmen and but few of those professing Whig principles took part in the proceedings,' and of the petition, 'it is evident that it originated with a section only of the town politically speaking.'[11] If incorporation was the expressed desire of radicalism then it was equally open to non-radical groups to express a public preference for the present pre-municipal system. Early in 1838 leading Conservatives organized a petition against incorporation which received 2,000 signatures but which was said to represent the wealth of the town. The Privy Council was left to adjudicate between property and numbers. (Gill, 1952, 225.)

THE BATTLE FOR AMALGAMATION

It eventually satisfied itself that a majority of ratepaying inhabitants did favour incorporation and a charter was granted in November 1838. Radicals and Liberals won every seat at the first election and they proceeded to elect a completely Liberal bench of aldermen and Liberal mayor, William Scholefield, the son of Birmingham's M.P. This radical triumph soon soured as the Council found itself assailed from all sides for its three supposed defects. First, its political complexion confirmed the view that Birmingham Town Council would be no more than the B.P.U. in permanent session. Its organizing core had in fact issued a list of favoured candidates before the election which smacked of dictation and which had to be hastily amended to meet local ward interests. In Manchester Tories had demonstrated their refusal to accept the legality of their charter by declining to participate in elections, but in Birmingham, though the grant of a charter was described as 'the most unconstitutional act that modern times has witnessed,' Tories did contest every ward, only to be completely routed. Their leaders were accused of 'vacillating conduct, inactivity and neglect' yet it did appear that Conservatives laboured under a severe handicap. The ward boundaries had been drawn favourable to radical interests, for it did seem strange that a party which claimed to have 1,200 of the largest ratepayers in the town should not gain even a single seat. A Tory propagandist explained why the ward arrangements were so important:

> Many of the Wards extend from the central to the outer parts of the town, forming most shapeless and unsightly figures; and it is hard to believe that such ingenuity in their formation and arrangement could be exercised for any other purpose than to combine a sufficient number of the smaller occupiers, in the remote parts of the town, to swamp the larger occupiers in the middle parts, amongst whom the Conservatives are chiefly to be found . . . the crowning instance is afforded by St Peter's Ward. Here will be found the most valuable property in the borough and the *elite* of the Conservative party, and if it had stood alone, or had been joined by any reasonable portion of the district around it, it would have inevitably returned Conservatives. This was averted by connecting it . . . with a large and distinct portion of the town.[12]

This was more than merely party propaganda excusing an electoral defeat, for even before the first election R. K. Douglas, editor of the radical *Birmingham Journal*, was relishing the way the Conservatives had been 'cribbed and cabined by ward divisions which have split up and mangled and minced their power without measure or mercy.'

Hence the radicalism of the Council alienated large sections of Birmingham opinion, which was confirmed in its prejudice by the second acclaimed municipal defect, the exclusive distribution of posts. Though Conservatives claimed to be shocked by the blatant spoils system which operated in 1839 such proceedings had been widely anticipated. Douglas had warned that municipal offices 'will be the gift of the Council — of the majority of the Council and the majority of the Council will not give their gift to neutrals, much less to opponents' while the leading Conservative editor perspectively identified the motive behind incorporation as 'personal aggrandisement . . . power and influence and some share of the loaves and fishes of official rank.'[13] The 'loaves and fishes' certainly went in one political direction as incorporation radicals received their rewards. William Redfern became Town Clerk, to be succeeded by his legal partner when he resigned; J. Birt Davies was elected coroner, forcing out the incumbent Tory. More controversially, R. K. Douglas, author of the Chartist National Petition, was appointed registrar in the mayor's court and the veteran radical George Edmonds became clerk of the peace. It has been argued that if the Conservatives had been allowed to retain the post of coroner (the office which in Manchester gave rise to the important legal case of *Rutter v Chapman*) their opposition to the Council might have moderated. Yet it was the appointment of Douglas and Edmonds to law enforcement posts which smothered any minimal Conservative sympathy for incorporation. This blatant expression of radical influence which effectively cocked a snook at normal convention deprived the Council of any vestige of dignity in Conservative eyes. Indeed it became a notorious mark of the Council's ineptitude and Peel encouraged Conservative disdain by asking in Parliament whether Tories 'could feel confidence in the exercise of local authority by a body which thought it consistent with its duty to make a delegate to the National Convention a registrar in the mayor's court?'.

This led naturally to the third ground for criticism — the Council could not be trusted to maintain law and order, hence should be deprived of control over the police. In June 1839 the Council drew up proposals for the levy of a rate specifically for the establishment of a police force. However, as a Conservative means of resisting incorporation, the overseers refused to levy the rate because of the doubtful legal validity of the charter. While thus immobilized the Council faced the threat of disorder from Chartists who had moved the National Convention to Birmingham. As a temporary expedient a troop of the Metropolitan Police was stationed in the town but they could not prevent (and may indeed have sparked off) the serious Bull Ring riots of July 1839. Attwood's persistent advocacy of peaceful protest and the previous withdrawal of the Birmingham delegates from the Convention could not prevent the Council's critics from spreading the dangerous libel that sympathy for the Chartist cause had induced the mayor and the municipal magistracy to tolerate lawless behaviour. These Chartist riots were the death knell to any hopes that Parliament would approve Russell's special legislation to allow Birmingham Town Council to set up a police force. Indeed Russell withdrew his bill and adopted Peel's suggestion that the Birmingham police force should be established under a special commissioner directly responsible to the Home Office. Birmingham was to pay for but not control a state police force and was thus to lose the one mandatory function of municipalities. It was a body blow at the very principle of municipal reform, and, as one citizen remarked, even forty years later the Police Act of 1839 could not be looked back upon 'without a feeling of shame and indignation and an ineradicable sense of wrong.'

For over a year the Council was in a humiliating state of suspended animation. Deprived of funds and powers it became effete. As a consequence public interest and councillors' attendance waned and the impression grew that the Council was an irrelevance in Birmingham affairs. It was to take many years to destroy this image. In November 1840 the Council resolved to break out of its strait jacket. Impatient of the delays in the crucial Manchester test case, the Council levied a borough rate and early in 1841 the overseers agreed to collect and deliver it. At last the Council could finance its limited activities. But still it was beset with difficulties. The county justices attempted to levy a county rate on the town, on the argument that the charter was illegal and Birmingham was still under the jurisdiction of the county bench. The justices were also in dispute with the Council over the prosecution of criminals at the quarter sessions and the maintenance of Birmingham prisoners at Warwick gaol. Finally the displaced Tory coroner was pursuing his claim for compensation, a case taken up in Parliament. The Council was prepared to fight all these attacks in the courts but in the event this was unnecessary. Peel's government unexpectedly came to the aid of the Council. First Graham, the Home Secretary, agreed that control of the police should revert to the Council in October 1842 and then the ministry introduced a bill to confirm the charters of incorporation for all three disputed towns, Birmingham, Manchester and Bolton. A hiatus of four years was over and the municipal history of Birmingham could now really begin. Perhaps the hopes of William Redfern would now be fulfilled. He had looked beyond the political role of corporations and anticipated a time when Parliament would confer upon the Council 'administrative powers of a local nature — such for instance as may be required for educational, statistical or sanitary purposes, or for the purpose of providing public walks and places of recreation.'[14]

Few at the time shared this vision of municipal social welfare, and the Council even in 1842 was ill-fitted to realize it. Confirmation of the legal authority of Birmingham Town Council did nothing to enhance its practical ability to govern the town. In particular there remained the problem of the competing jurisdiction of rival administrative bodies. The Birmingham Street Commission was the most important of these but its authority was limited to the parish of Birmingham. There were also administrative bodies in the parishes of Aston and Edgbaston, both within the borough, and township authorities in Bordesley, Deritend and Duddeston-cum-Nechells. In all there were eight separate administrative but non-municipal agencies in the town. Some had assumed that incorporation would automatically lead to 'the consolidation of the entire of the local acts and the concentration of the powers granted by them in one body and their administration by one set of officers.' Yet though this was possible by voluntary arrangement a Tory critic noted sharply that the Council did not 'sufficiently possess the confidence of the other public bodies having municipal powers to induce them to transfer those powers to the Town Council under the Municipal Act.'[15] There was no alternative: the battle for confirmation would have to be followed by the battle for amalgamation.

Just as the *Birmingham Journal* had been the propaganda mouthpiece for incorporation, so it was also the publicist for amalgamation, though under different editorship. R. K. Douglas had been the Council's great champion during his editorship from 1836 to 1844, and his successor J. A. Jaffray proclaimed the need for amalgamation of powers as soon as he took over the paper. In May, 1844, Jaffray launched an amalgamation campaign against the 'Babel of confusion' in Birmingham local government which was to last until his goal was achieved in 1851. He received support from an unexpected quarter, for the question was also taken up by the *Midland Counties Herald*, an advertising paper that had previously eschewed any editorial opinions. Despite this strong press lobby for amalgamation, the old parochial and township institutions had their defenders. One Tory supporter remarked in 1845 that 'we do not fear to trust a body of men who have so well performed their duties . . . and who though not *called a representative* body are really composed of and represent every important party and interest in the borough' and when the Birmingham street commissioners appeared threatened by national sanitary legislation they were stoutly defended as a body 'fully competent to exercise their powers . . . and deserving of better treatment than to be hastily superseded.'[16] As if to demonstrate their vitality, both the surveyors of Duddleston-cum-Nechells and the Birmingham Street Commission promoted their own improvement bills in 1845, though town meetings overwhelmingly favoured amalgamation of these bodies in the Town Council.

Yet radicals were also unhappy about such a process. They feared that without an extension of the suffrage 'centralized despotism and irresponsible power' would be placed solely 'in the hands of the wealthy and leave the poor without the slightest means of protecting themselves against local oppression.' Here was a hint of that radical opposition to incorporation that Birmingham politics had previously cloaked. The 'tyranny of the bloated rich' would express itself through amalgamation, and therefore the radical answer was to liberalize rather than centralize the township institutions. Instead of one municipal leviathan, radicals wanted small discrete district representative bodies which, elected on universal suffrage, would secure 'the social and sanatory well being of the community.' As we shall see later on, this was a possibility explored in Sheffield in the 1850s. Such fragmentation of local government did not attract Birmingham Liberal opinion and the Duddeston separatist move was roundly criticized by Jaffray:

> Before long Duddeston and Nechells will be what they unquestionably ought to be, an integral municipal part of the Borough of Birmingham. The inhabitants of a district who share in the advantage of a common municipal government and who also participate in the Parliamentary franchise have no right to pick and choose what common burthens they will accept or repudiate.[17]

What gave an added cutting edge to the amalgamation campaign was Birmingham's worsening sanitary condition. A co-ordinated rather than a competitive local government system would be both cheaper and more efficient; but its main advantage was that it would permit a unified sanitary policy on such things as drainage. Birmingham's natural advantages were yielding to population growth and overcrowding, and doctors and clergymen advertised the sanitary problems associated with the squalor and disease of working-class districts. As usual municipal reform became sanitary administration and so amalgamation and public health naturally coalesced in support of the 1848 Public Health Act. Once it appeared that the strong expression of town opinion in favour of amalgamation was going to meet with no response from the entrenched bodies, the Council turned to an order under the new act which would impose amalgamation from above. When Lord Morpeth's bill was first introduced it was welcomed in Birmingham because 'it will sweep away the hydra-headed authority that taxes the inhabitants in a hundred different shapes and through a dozen different agencies'; and when the Act finally passed it was received as a measure 'by which the principle of amalgamation will be directly promoted.' The Council next sponsored a petition for an inspection by the General Board of Health, created by the 1848 Act, in the hope of securing an order under the Public Health Act designating the Council as the local board of health. Amalgamation would thus come by administrative precept rather than by the consent of the commissioners.

In 1849 the Board's inspector, Robert Rawlinson, reported on the sanitary condition of the town. Though Birmingham was healthier than many large towns, its death rate of 26.5 per thousand was still high and Rawlinson had no difficulty in demonstrating the lack of basic sanitary amenities in the town. He recommended a speedy application of the Public Health Act which could improve health and raise the moral condition of Birmingham:

1. By a perfect system of street, court, yard and house drainage.
2. By a constant and cheap supply of pure water under pressure, laid on to every house and yard, to the entire superseding of all local wells and pumps, the water of which is impure.
3. By the substitution of water-closets or soil pan apparatus (for the more expensive existing privies and cesspools) with proper drains to carry away all surface water and refuse from the roofs, streets, yards and water-closets.
4. By properly paved courts and passages, and by a regular system of washing and cleansing all courts, passages, footpaths, and surface channels.[18]

These improvements could be secured only by a unified sanitary management, and the report was full of comments on the need for consolidation of all powers in the Town Council as the local board of health. The Council could not have asked for a stronger recommendation for amalgamation and an order to that effect was expected.

Chadwick's notorious insensitivity now disrupted the procedure. Without allowing due time for consulting local interests (there were over a dozen submissions made in protest at Rawlinson's report) Birmingham was included in a bill enforcing the Board of Health's provisional order. The Birmingham Street Commission led the protests at this highhanded action, though some saw this as merely an excuse for general opposition. As Jaffray perceived, 'the Commissioners . . . have taken advantage of a technical informality in the Bill . . . to get up a display of hostility ostensibly against the informality but really against the measure which will transfer their powers to a properly elected body.'[19] Even many who favoured amalgamation were hostile to central inspection and control, notably the great anti-centralization pundit Joshua Toulmin Smith, himself a Birmingham property owner. Toulmin Smith presented a petition against applying the 1848 Act to Birmingham and wrote a series of powerful articles in a new paper, the *Birmingham Mercury*. In them he made it quite clear that he was no reactionary defender of the various commissions but a supporter of the ratepayers:

> We asserted their clear right to one responsible representative body to manage their affairs . . . We must not have our irresponsible local bodies amalgamated. What we must have . . . is the *replacement* of all these irresponsible bodies by one single representative body—the Town Council. The Commissioners must not form an alliance with the Town Council: but *all* the power of *all* Commissioners and local boards must be vested in the Town Council.[20]

Yet if this were to be achieved through 'surrender to an irresponsible distant jobbing clique,' such as the General Board of Health, this would be too high a price to pay. Representative local self government could not be sacrificed to centralization.

The outcry was sufficient to secure the withdrawal of Birmingham from the 1849 list, and so the Council renewed its request for an order in 1850. By then it was once more at loggerheads with the Street Commission, which promoted its own bill. There was a possibility of joint action between the two contending parties, but the Commission wished to create a sanitary authority for a natural drainage district to include areas outside the borough while the Council was adamant for full and sole municipal control. The Commission mustered enough powerful voices to persuade the General Board of Health to drop Birmingham again, and the Council was frustrated once more, this time only temporarily. The growing overlap in membership between the Council and the Commission provided a launching pad for a compromise, worked out largely by Henry Smith, a mayor in 1845-6 and 1851-2 but formerly a street commissioner. A jointly sponsored Improvement Act could provide all the sanitary and administrative advantages of a Public Health Act order without the disadvantages of centralization. The Birmingham Improvement Act of 1851 vested all powers previously exercised by local commissioners in the Town Council, which was also endowed with some new powers. (Gill, 1952, 358). The Council was from 1 January 1852 the sole authority for roads, sewers, lighting, street improvement and public buildings. It had avoided central inspection and direction, but that concession had been bought by stricter financial limits on enforced improvements to property. The Public Health Act would have given greater powers to press property owners reluctant to make sanitary improvements, so in this sense the 1851 Act was a compromise both between the Council and the Commissions and between sanitary reformers and property owners.

FALSE STARTS—REACTION BEFORE ACHIEVEMENT

Birmingham Town Council arrived in 1852 at that position reached in Leeds in 1842 and in Liverpool in 1847 where it could become a reforming sanitary institution. Without local rivals, its prestige would be enhanced and it could now provide a natural location for the exercise of authority by the town's economic elite. That it fulfilled neither of these functions in the next fifteen years or so was largely due to the parsimony that gripped Council affairs in the 1850s and 1860s. Some had sensed this danger, and as early as 1852 a zealous doctor had warned against false economies:

> The Town Council, by the Act of Amalgamation has now full power . . . but from . . . a growing disposition to economize I fear many important measures will be either overlooked or neglected. We all wish for economy and small rates, — they constitute the *eclat* of some public men —, but cutting down rates to the lowest possible sum, and omitting sanatary regulations lead to other expenses, which may more than equal the saving. —a judicious expenditure is as much required as a judicious economy of the public money.[21]

The story of municipal economy in mid-Victorian Birmingham is essentially the story of two men, Joseph Allday and Thomas Avery, Allday the high priest of the 1850s and Avery of the 1860s.

Allday was a remarkable political activist who had first become known as a Tory-radical in the later 1820s, when he ran a scurrilous propaganda sheet, the *Argus*. He delighted in seeking out devious doings by public men and his greatest coup came in 1853 when he exposed scandalous prison malpractice, which became the subject of government enquiry and prosecution. This was the base from which he launched an economist campaign of stunning ferocity. He became a councillor in 1849 and was supported both inside the Council and beyond by small tradesmen, shopkeepers and clerks. It was a municipal revolt by the petty bourgeoisie, inured by occupation to meagreness. They were 'the unprogressive tradesmen class . . . not accustomed to deal with big transactions and high figures, so that spending large sums of money, if proposed, filled the brewer, the baker and the candlestick maker with alarm.' A simple recital of events in the 1850s will provide clear indication of the nature of Allday's municipal regime.

Things began well enough in 1852 with the appointment of committees and the commencement of the major new projects of sewerage and street improvement. As ever, the estimates for both fell short of the expenditure, and within a year there was a deficit and a need to increase both the rating and borrowing limits of the 1851 Act. In the spring of 1853 the 'economist' din was first heard. In March Allday led a determined attempt to reduce the rates; in April ratepayers presented a memorial expressing alarm at the borough finances; and in June the Council agreed to appoint a committee to secure cuts in borough expenditure. From now on the Council, politically united in radical-Liberalism, was divided between an 'economist' and an 'extravagant' party (Briggs, 1963, 214). The latter was by no means overwhelmed, and it took up the two important questions of public control of water supply and new improvement powers. The municipal purchase of the Birmingham Waterworks Company established in 1826 had been envisaged in the 1851 Improvement Act and when the company secured new powers to extend their works in 1854, the Council decided to draft proposals to complete the purchase. Surveys were commissioned and a bill prepared by the general purposes committee. Ratepayers presented petitions against the purchase and in December 1854 a majority was gained in the Council for the rejection of the bill, thus delaying public ownership for twenty years. Exactly a year later Allday achieved his greatest triumph in the abandonment of the proposed Improvement Act. When in November 1855 the Council approved further legislation to finance sewerage and street improvement, Allday, supported by the Ratepayers' Protection Society, succeeded in making the Parliamentary application subject to the consent of a town meeting. This occurred in December 1855, at the noisiest public meeting in Birmingham for years. Allday's motion to refuse the Council permission to go ahead was carried by acclamation and a subsequent town poll supported his stance by a margin of twenty to one. Without the prospect of new funds from increased borrowing powers and higher rates, the Corporation's bankers refused to finance any more expenditure (the overdraft was already £26,000), whereupon the public works and finance committees resigned *en bloc*. 'Economists' filled their places and Allday became chairman of both committees. There was an immediate brake on municipal activities, and as a consequence, expenditure by the public works department fell by a third between 1853 and 1858.

In such an atmosphere of retrenchment there was friction between the political masters bent on economy and municipal officials anxious to fulfil their responsibilities. The honorary medical officer requested that he be allowed to make *weekly* returns of deaths, but permission was refused, although it would cost a paltry £75 per year. When this doctor resigned in protest, the Council decided not to fill his position, since they judged that his duties could be adequately performed by an inspector of nuisances. The Council was in dispute with its town clerk over his fees and municipal duties, with its treasurer and with the recorder who favoured a stipendiary magistrate, a post the Council refused to sanction. By far the most important of these disputes was the vendetta conducted by Allday against the borough surveyor James Pigott Smith, who had given many years of sterling service to the Street Commission prior to the amalgamation. Refusing to accept quietly the constraints upon his functions imposed by the economists, Pigott Smith was eventually dismissed in 1857 and replaced by his docile deputy at half his salary. These and other municipal rows were highly personalized and bitterly fought out. Insults abounded, tempers rose and frequently very minor points became hotly contested. In 1858 three whole days of wrangling were needed to settle the membership of Council committees and resignations of individuals and committees were common. Council proceedings became a byword for faction and pot-house politics. Allday and his cronies held forth in the Old Woodman Tavern and this period was known as the era of the 'old Woodman Council.' It thus appears as something of a mockery that the Queen in her perambulation of the great cities conferred a knighthood on the mayor in 1858.

Better days were soon at hand. Allday had made many enemies and in 1859 he was defeated at the aldermanic elections. Feeling bitterly betrayed, he resigned from the Council and the economists lost their main political protagonist. In any case circumstances were enforcing a more positive municipal policy. The Council was faced with an injunction against pumping untreated sewage into the river Tame and so had to provide the means of filtration. At the turn of the decade the extravagant party made the running with the financial expertise of Robert Wright (an accountant elected in 1858), the reform enthusiasm of Henry Hawkes (a former mayor), and the improvement experience of the solicitor Arthur Rylands (a former street commissioner who had originally advocated amalgamation by private act, and who was mayor in the crucial year 1860-1). In these circumstances the renewed attempt to gain another Improvement Act became something of a test of opinion on municipal affairs. In December 1860 a town meeting reversed the decision of five years earlier, and by a vote of nearly two to one authorized the Council to seek new powers. The Improvement Act of 1861 raised the Corporation's borrowing limit for general works (including sewerage) to £300,000 and for street improvements to £150,000. There were also powers for stricter building regulations and for smoke control.

Birmingham Town Council was still in the trammels of 'economists,' though now of a different variety. In 1862 Thomas Avery, a partner in the famous scales firm, entered the Council and for the latter part of the decade he was its moving spirit. Avery saw the fundamental weaknesses of Allday's negative parsimony. Simple retrenchment often led to inefficiency without necessarily avoiding expenditure. For instance, the Council inherited from the Street Commission a legal obligation to complete a new street. When, as a cost-cutting measure, the Council refused to do so, it was sued and had to pay compensation to the aggrieved parties, although eventually the street was laid out. Avery therefore favoured a policy of economy allied to efficiency. While public money should not be wasted, it could nevertheless be spent wisely in promoting efficient municipal activities. At the same time the salutary constraints imposed by ratepaying opinion must not be dissolved by administrative devices. It was for this reason that Avery joined the guardians of the poor in a legal action to prevent the Council's taking advantage of the Municipal Mortgages Act of 1860. Under this Act Councils could borrow and enlarge their borough debt simply with Treasury approval. In Birmingham this was controversial because it bypassed the town meeting of ratepayers which economists had always used to restrain a potentially extravagant Council. Having put municipal finances on a sounder footing by reform of accounting procedures, Avery still wished to retain the consent of the ratepayers as a control over municipal expenditure. His approach to municipal policy was vividly exposed in a public pronouncement he made in 1865. The great annual meeting of intellectual societies were always the occasion for reviews of municipal progress. When the Social Science Association met in Liverpool in 1858 the borough engineer James Newlands had proudly examined the Council's sanitary policy. It was in a very different vein that Avery addressed the British Association meeting in 1865 when he concluded:

1. That the progress of the town in wealth and population has been enormous but that the amount of taxation and of municipal expenditure has increased in still greater proportions.
2. That the public debt especially appears to have increased excessively owing to the rapidity with which public works and various improvements have been executed thereby imposing heavy burdens upon the present generation of ratepayers.
3. That it would have been desirable to have omitted some of the least important of these undertakings and to have extended the others over a longer period of time and that for the future they should either be suspended altogether or proceeded with more slowly and deliberately.[22]

Ironically, as it turned out, Avery was himself the instigator of the abandonment of this cautious approach. By the end of the 1860s renewed difficulties over sewage disposal forced Avery to take a stand against the inefficiencies of the public works committee which could only be remedied by a more positive policy. Furthermore, on the question of water supply, in 1869 Avery strongly advocated full municipal control, arguing that 'it is the duty of a wise local government to endeavour to surround the humbler classes of the population with its benevolent and protecting care.' (Avery, 1869, 14) This was indeed a new canon on the school of economy, and it demonstrates that Avery, himself a Congregationalist, had been influenced by that 'civic gospel' being dispensed by

Birmingham Nonconformist ministers in the 1860s. It was the civic gospel which underlay the great flowering of Birmingham municipal government in the 1870s (Hennock, 1973, 61–79).

THE CIVIC GOSPEL

In reviewing the body of thought that flowed from mid-Victorian Birmingham and transformed the very idea of municipal government, elevating it to a new plane of achievement and potential, two important points should be made. First, Birmingham was notoriously backward in its municipal administration before 1870, and the 'civic renaissance' which was to occur after that date, associated with the mayoralty of Joseph Chamberlain, in many ways merely repaired omissions rather than made innovations. The questions of sewerage and improvement, the public ownership of gas and water and the establishment of the social status of the Council had all featured in the municipal history of other towns long before Chamberlain entered the Council. Birmingham was thus well behind other towns, and in energetically seeking to catch up, it then found itself at the head of the municipal league. The second point is that the Birmingham civic gospel was itself not wholly original, though it had never been so clearly stated or so coherently thought through. We have already noticed how a number of municipal reformers gradually struggled towards the idea of the Council as the guardian of the welfare of the local community. As responsibility for environmental control was acknowledged (for strong pragmatic rather than philosophical reasons), ideas about the wider responsibilities that councils might adopt had inevitably followed. The Birmingham civic gospel built on these scattered notions to create a very philosophy of municipal government.

The initial conception of this philosophy owed much to the actual municipal history of Birmingham. Initially because of its radicalism and later because of its factionalism, the Birmingham Town Council had been shunned by the urban elite.

Those who wished to elevate the Council's role had first to make it socially acceptable and this was done by making political and local government responsibility a religious imperative. In the 1860s the Birmingham bourgeoisie learnt from the pulpit that they had a religious duty to serve the needs of their fellow men and the local environment determined how those needs could be met. Interestingly enough, at about the same time in Liverpool the merchant princes were also being advised on their spiritual and religious duties. Since in Liverpool there was already a great tradition of municipal service, there the new humanitarian drive was directed towards philanthropy. In Birmingham the elite had always sponsored charitable activities and the deficiency was municipal. Hence late Victorian Liverpool was noted for its philanthropic, and Birmingham for its municipal zeal.

The civic gospel was largely the creation of two Nonconformist ministers George Dawson and R. W. Dale, both of whom were inspiring speakers. Dawson had come to Birmingham as a Baptist minister in 1844 and soon set up his own unorthodox congregation, the Church of the Saviour. For almost thirty years he weekly addressed varied assemblies at his church on the civil duties of man. He was far more concerned with practical behaviour than with specific doctrinal creed and he stressed the religious obligation for his followers to serve their city and cater to its needs. Above all, he was concerned with the salvation of education and its society-wide appeal, which for many of his disciples was the main motive for entering municipal service. Dawson translated the values and obligations of the church to the corporation, which became the modern expression of God's will. In his view the Council occupied a parallel position to the state: 'A great town exists to discharge towards the people of that town the duties that a great nation exists to discharge towards the people of that nation.' Municipal collectivism thus became the new religion. Some found this theologically near-heretical, and the more orthodox dissenters looked instead to Robert Dale, a Congregationalist minister in Birmingham for over forty years. Dale had been much influenced by Dawson, though he did not share his religious view of what constituted a modern church. What he did stress was the need to do God's work in civil life, above all in politics. Some dissenters had found the acrimony of political conflict alien to their religious beliefs; and to this had been added a middle-class distaste of the hurly-burly of popular politics. Dale stridently dismissed both, urging his middle-class nonconformist followers to take municipal power in order to 'see to it that the towns and parishes in which they live are well drained, well lighted and well paved.' Dale and Dawson were thus preaching a gospel in which municipal service and political activism were intrinsically part of a religious mission. The character and goals of local government were thereby elevated and Dale portrayed the transformation which took place in Birmingham:

> Towards the end of the sixties a few Birmingham men made the discovery that perhaps a strong and able Town Council might do almost as much to improve conditions of life in the town as Parliament itself . . . They spoke of sweeping away streets in which it was not possible to live a healthy and decent life; of making the town cleaner, sweeter, brighter; of providing gardens parks and a museum; they insisted that great monopolies like the gas and water supply should be in the hands of the corporation.[23]

Such ideas could not be translated simply from the mouths of Dawson and Dale straight into reality, for there was the always vital question of achieving municipal power to pursue policy goals. Municipal reformers in Birmingham showed that they were vitally aware of this. In order to ripen public opinion they established their own satirical newspaper, *The Town Crier*, which contrasted the Council's bold potential with its shabby achievement. One of the paper's moving spirits was William Harris, a devoted follower of Dawson, and it was Harris who created the political machine known as the 'caucus' which transformed late Victorian urban politics. A systematized political device based on ward organization, the caucus was devised first to meet the problems of a mass electorate and the minority clause of 1867* and later to resolve the difficulties of

*This provision of the Second Reform Act gave large cities a third seat in Parliament, while restricting voters to two votes. It was intended to represent a town's minority interest, but in Birmingham the Liberal Caucus was able to return three M.P.s by disciplined voting.

the cumulative voting for school boards. It was easily applied to the local elections for town councillor and guardian and gave to the Liberal party a great political advantage in local affairs. Party political rivalries were intensified in a way that was quite novel in Birmingham life and since Liberalism was now endowed with a coherent municipal programme the issues of local government became the very stuff of local politics.

In the 1870s Birmingham's civic renaissance had four main planks, sewerage, gas, water and improvement. They were all to figure prominently in the mayoralty of Joseph Chamberlain, who executed the new municipal ideology of Dawson, Dale and his own unitarian pastor H. W. Crosskey (Briggs, 1952, 67–9). The new dimensions in municipal policy first emerged in 1870 with Avery's intervention into the question of sewage disposal. Faced with legal action yet again, the Corporation through its public works committee, proposed to purchase a huge area for the establishment of a sewage farm. The committee's proposals became a major political controversy and Avery put himself at the head of those opposing the sewage farm who included all of the newer municipal recruits inspired by the civic gospel anxious to end the sad story of inefficiency. Between April and July 1871 Avery secured the appointment of a special Council committee with himself as chairman to review the sewage question. This was a vote of no confidence in the public works committee and marks the accession to power of positive municipal Liberalism. The days of economy, of both the new and the old variety, were very much over, for the dawn of the civic renaissance was at hand. The sewage committee's report, though hotly debated, was accepted by 33 to 23 in October and this committee was put in charge of the new arrangements, a great political coup for the reformers and a blow at the prestige of public works committee. By the removal of 14,000 open privy middens and associated cesspools, the adoption of the pan system of sewage collection and disposal, and the removal of nuisances caused by the outflow of sewage into waterways the sewage committee had considerably ameliorated Birmingham's sewerage problems, and in 1875 the Court of Chancery pronounced itself satisfied.

It was in the course of Avery's historic report in October 1871 that the first serious evidence on differential death rates within the borough was accumulated. Only then was it gradually realized that the favourable overall borough death rate hid the true extent of sanitary problems in certain districts. The sewerage question was thus of sharp relevance to the issue of mortality and morbidity and it was this dimension which was taken up by Chamberlain who became Mayor in November 1873, and was re-elected in the two subsequent years. Only when forced to do so by national legislation did Birmingham appoint a medical officer of health in 1872. For three years the Council refused to accept a central government grant towards his salary for fear of loss of local autonomy. The Liberal political thrust which carried Chamberlain to the mayoralty also delivered the sanitary committee into the hands of reformers, whose public health policy was to be directed by William Cook for the next thirty years. Cook, as Chamberlain's sanitary lieutenant, organized a sanitary survey of the town in 1874–5, which exposed once and for all the fallacy of Birmingham as a supremely healthy city. Cook's sanitary committee reported in February 1875 that improved public health depended upon three things: sewerage, paving, and scavenging supported by regular inspection. Whereas Birmingham had only one health inspector to every 30,000 the committee proposed an increase in manpower to one for every 10,000. There was to be a new programme of classification of houses according to condition, the worst of which required weekly inspection. When Cook moved the motion to introduce the new sanitary regime he was opposed by the uncouth William Brinsley, a grocer and property owner, who was Birmingham's equivalent to the Leeds 'economist' Archie Scarr. Brinsley denounced the principle of regular house inspection as 'unconstitutional and un-English' and protested that citizens would lose 'that which has hitherto been held most dear to Englishmen—namely the sanctity of domestic life.' Brinsley's fierce rearguard action was defeated and the new regulations were introduced. Hence by 1875 the combined effects of improved sewerage facilities and tighter inspection created a healthier sanitary environment, which by the beginning of the 1880s made substantial inroads into the death rate (Bunce, 1885, 110–26).

Improved sanitary management always carried the sting in the tail of increased municipal expenditure and it appeared that the Chamberlainite revolution might be stopped in its tracks because of resistance to increased rates. During Chamberlain's first year of office a town meeting rejected the adoption of general public health legislation which would have removed the financial limit on improvement rates specified in Birmingham's local acts. As a direct consequence, in March 1874 improvement estimates had to be reduced by £41,000 to keep within the local rating ceiling. It was thus a great financial breakthrough for the Corporation to purchase the two gas companies and apply the profits to subsidize municipal expenditure. This was Chamberlain's bold venture and his first act as mayor. As early as January 1874 he persuaded the Council to approve in principle the municipalization of gas supply. Throughout the long negotiations and the tortuous path of Parliamentary legislation Chamberlain stuck by his prophecy that there would be great economies through municipal management, great efficiency and above all public profits. He anticipated an annual profit of £14,000 rising to £50,000 within fourteen years, and this alone was sufficient to silence opposition. There were, moreover, important questions of principle involved, the question of monopoly and the role of corporations. Chamberlain told the Council:

> I distinctly hold that all monopolies which are sustained in any way by the State ought to be in the hands of the representatives of the people —by the representative authority should they be administered, and to them should their profits go and not to private speculators . . . I am inclined to increase the duties and responsibilities of the local authority . . . and will do everything in my power to constitute these local authorities real local parliaments, supreme in their special jurisdiction.[24]

Municipal gas supply would thus enhance the municipal ideal. When the bill authorizing the purchase finally went through Parliament in 1875 Chamberlain moved and Avery seconded the appointment of a gas committee. It was a symbol of the bridge between the old economy and the new extravagance.

The issue of municipal gas went hand in hand with that of municipal water, and again this linked Avery and Chamberlain. The fullest case for municipal control based largely on health grounds had been put in Avery's pamphlet in 1869, in which he asserted that it was the duty of the council 'to consider the general welfare of all classes of the population.' Nothing came of his initiative largely because the private company was not interested in negotiating. It required Chamberlain's zeal and political drive to push the purchase through and he took up the question in December 1874 when the political will had been generated by the gas question. Municipal gas was the result of Chamberlain's first year as mayor, municipal water, of the second. Gas was largely a question of money, water of health. Chamberlain delivered a three pronged attack upon the water issue. He argued, first, that water supply was vital to health and that Birmingham's worsening death rates made improved supplies vital; second, that only a corporation could adequately meet the community's needs since the private company was primarily responsible for making profits for its shareholders; and third, that rapid inflation in the company's stock value made immediate action vital. There was no disagreement on the proposal to purchase the water company and Chamberlain was unanimously supported in the Council and at a ratepayers' meeting. Only the company resisted on the grounds that compulsory purchase would be unfair in view of the successful record of supplying the town with water. In Parliament the company's interests were vigorously defended and in presenting evidence in favour of the corporation Chamberlain and Avery stressed the health aspect. The former told the Comons 'the power of life and death should not be left in the hands of a commercial company but should be conducted by the representatives of the people' and the latter advised the Lords that the Corporation would have the 'duty . . . to consider how a much larger supply of pure and wholesome water can be obtained for purely sanitary purposes, without regard to commercial results at all.' Public health triumphed over private commerce and the bill went through. On exactly the same date, 2 August 1875, the royal assent was given to the Birmingham Corporation's gas and water bills, establishing the city as a centre of municipal collectivism, or as it was soon to be called, 'gas and water socialism.'

Chamberlain's crowning achievement was still to come and it required all the strength of his dynamic personality to push through what he neatly termed a piece of 'sagacious audacity.' The Conservative's Artisans' Dwellings Act of 1875 extended the powers of corporation to acquire, clear and redevelop urban slum areas. Chamberlain, who had been consulted by Home Secretary Cross during the Act's passage, was determined that Birmingham should embark upon a programme under the Act and his scheme was characteristically bold. The 'Improvement Scheme' was presented to the Council in October 1875. It envisaged a wholesale redevelopment of Birmingham city centre, involving the purchase of ninety three acres at a cost of £1.3m (and this followed the expenditure of about £3m on the gas and water undertakings). The scheme rested firmly upon sanitary considerations. The M.O.H. designated an area of St. Mary's Ward as unsanitary and required that its properties be demolished. Their condition was movingly described by the ward councillor, William White, a Quaker philanthropist and chairman of the Council's improvement committee:

> Little else is to be seen but bowing roofs, tottering chimneys, tumbledown and often disused shopping, heaps of bricks, broken windows, rough pavements damp and sloppy. It is not easy to describe the dreary desolation which acre after acre of the very heart of the town presents . . . completely given over to misery and squalor . . . if it were possible with safety to the lives of the inhabitants the very best and cheapest thing to do would be to burn it clean down.[25]

Such qualitative evidence could be underpinned with one vital statistic—the death rate in St. Mary's was double that in bourgeois Edgbaston. To the sanitary dimension of the slum clearance scheme Chamberlain added town improvement. A wide boulevard was to be laid out, opening up the cramped city centre, to enhance the appearance, augment the shopping facilities and facilitate the traffic of the town. This major undertaking was possible only because of the recruitment to the Council of substantial entrepreneurs like Chamberlain with the necessary business acumen. Indeed a group of them set up a trust to purchase properties in the designated areas even before Parliament had approved the Birmingham scheme.

This was the most controversial of Chamberlain's plans, and it led to the most acrimonious party controversy. When the Local Government Board inspector held his local enquiry the Conservatives used every device to discredit the scheme. As one of them recalled, 'they fought the scheme tooth and nail . . . they contrived and schemed at every turn to wreck it . . . it was vile and ruinous and pernicious and wicked and against the constitution and the scriptures.' By the time Parliament had finally given its consent, Chamberlain himself had become an M.P. and resigned as mayor. He could write his own municipal epitaph: 'I think I have now almost completed my municipal programme . . . The town will be parked, paved, assized, marketed, gas and watered and *improved* — all as a result of three years' active work.' There was audacity in the Improvement Scheme and things did not go well in the depressed years of the 1880s but the new street was laid out and by 1885 Bunce, editor of the *Daily Post* and a strong Chamberlainite, was able to assess its impact:

> Driving a broad roadway through what was once the most crowded, the poorest and the most insanitary quarter of the town, seems to have carried light, and air, and life throughout the district. Slums and rookeries, pestilential morally and physically, have disappeared as if by magic, and have given place to streets and buildings worthy of occupying the centre of a great town, while other portions of the improvement area have been so benefited and purified that an artisan population may now occupy them without injury to health or the sacrifice of self-respect.[26]

The new street was appropriately named Corporation Street, a fitting tribute to the new corporate horizons opened up during Chamberlain's mayoralty. The ripples in the municipal pool were seen far beyond Birmingham, for the civic gospel and the Chamberlainite civic renaissance to which it gave rise left their indelible mark upon English municipal history. No man had ever before enshrined municipal service with such noble sentiments, and by so doing Chamberlain had elevated the whole tone of municipal life. Three days before resigning as Mayor Chamberlain expressed the municipal ideal:

> For my part I have an abiding faith in municipal institutions, an abiding sense of the value and importance of local government and I desire therefore to surround them by everything which can mark their importance, which can show the place they occupy in public estimation and respect, and which can point to their great value to the community. Our corporation represents the authority of the people.[27]

The Birmingham Town Council was responsible for, said Chamberlain, 'the welfare, the health, the comfort and the lives of 400,000 people.' Municipal reform could have no finer goal than that.

Five
Bristol, Leicester, Bradford and Sheffield

The municipal progress thus far charted has been in the great cities of Victorian England. It is important to enquire whether a similar pattern occurred in the towns of lesser rank. It has already been noticed that England's local government system included both corporate and unincorporated towns, the latter being governed by parochial authorities, the county bench and, increasingly, local boards. The corporate towns were themselves marked by divisions, for instance between the industrial metropolis like Birmingham and the small market or cathedral town like York. Between these two lay the towns with substantial urban spread and population growth, but which did not quite come into the category of the metropolitan city. Four of these — Bristol, Leicester, Bradford and Sheffield — are briefly surveyed here. The last named was the nearest in size to the great cities and it exceeded 200,000 population in the 1860s; Bristol followed suit in the 1870s, Bradford in the 1880s and Leicester in the 1890s. There were interesting similarities and differences among these four towns. Two, Bristol and Leicester, had ancient corporations which bequeathed to their reformed councils a crushing burden of debt. Both towns adopted the 1848 Public Health Act. The other two, Bradford and Sheffield, were unincorporated towns and they received their charters of incorporation in the 1840s. Both preferred to work with private local acts rather than national sanitary legislation, though neither was to be successful in so doing. The four covered a range of economic interests. Bristol was a port, Leicester a hosiery and textile town, Bradford was England's worsted capital and Sheffield was the archetypal iron and steel town.

Bristol, Leicester, Bradford and Sheffield

These four, along with Liverpool, Leeds and Birmingham, accounted for a large section of England's nineteenth century economy.

BRISTOL

Until the late eighteenth century Bristol had been England's third largest town, and her corporation, dating back to medieval times, was secured by royal charter of 1373. The growth of the Atlantic trade had boosted the town's position, and Bristol, because of its port and westward location, had grown fat on the proceeds of slaves and sugar. Influence in Bristol was shared between the commercial interest — as expressed by the renowned Society of Merchant Venturers, the private enterprise of the Dock Company, which managed Bristol's main economic asset — and the Corporation, the town's largest property owner. This division was, however, more apparent than real, for the Corporation was enmeshed with the other two bodies through common membership, and with other local government institutions such as the select vestries and the Poor Law agency, the Incorporation of the Poor. Sustained by life membership and co-option the members of the Corporation operated as the public expression of the elite of Bristol society.

In the eighteenth century the Corporation had been predominantly Whig, but in 1812 the Tories gained control, which was soon secured by a policy of exclusive party nominations for aldermen. As we shall see, it was a regime which was to last for a century. As a parliamentary borough Bristol was ideally placed for the exercise of corporate influence, and many a borough of this sort was little more than a nomination seat for the local corporation. Bristol Corporation, unlike that at Leicester, did not, in fact, exercise undue influence in parliamentary elections. Neither by partial creation of freemen nor by bribery and corruption did the Corporation seek to make its political predilection manifest at election time. Bristol was not to be indicted on the Municipal Commission's charge that 'the perversion of Municipal institutions to political ends had occasioned the sacrifice of local interest to party purpose.'

On many other aspects of the deficiencies of the unreformed system Bristol had not such clean hands (Bush, 1976, 42–71). Its administration of charities had been, to say the least, lax, and when the Corporation was reformed a complex web of mismanagement, fraud and betrayal was revealed. Its record on maintenance of law and order was far from impressive at the end of its life. In the 1820s the borough courts had been subject to radical criticism and in 1831 the Corporation was at the very heart of the row over the famous Bristol riots, which ensued when the House of Lords rejected the second version of the Reform Bill. The suppression of the riots was the responsibility of the bench of magistrates at whose head was the mayor, who was tried for dereliction of duty but acquitted. The origin of and dispute over the riots were very confused but they displayed considerable public antipathy towards the Corporation, and the whole episode may have been directed towards discrediting the Corporation and supporting the case for reform (Thomas, 1974, 12). The police force was reformed as a result and the Corporation faced a bill of £55,000 for compensation, another debt to be bequeathed to its successor.

Yet the main defect of Bristol Corporation was that, like others, it was intrinsically remote from its community whose welfare it largely ignored. Because of its exclusiveness the Corporation had no popular base, and because of its own properties it was geared to private rather than public functions. Its highest priority was the maintenance of its own interests through the management of its own properties, and its attitude has been well paraphrased by its modern historian:

> As an essentially private body our first charge is to administer our inherited assets and affairs as we deem fit, not subject to outside scrutiny or external direction . . . the public have no legitimate access to either our deliberations or our funds. . . . But . . . provided our rights are not at risk we will endeavour to promote the city's interests. It must be expressly understood that we reject the notion of being answerable to any body of people other than ourselves.[1]

It is hardly surprising that the most serious charge levelled by the Corporation Commissioners was that Bristol Corporation had failed to arrest the decline of the port while spending money on conspicuous consumption. Yet the Corporation itself believed that it was being accused of neglecting a public responsibility which it did not acknowledge. Its first loyalty was to itself and not to the town.

Predictably, it fought hard to resist reform and spent £400 in lobbying Parliament in order to exclude Bristol from the bill. It sold off £8,000 of property in its last year, but unlike similar manoeuvres in Leeds and Liverpool, this was aimed at financial rather than political objectives. The Corporation's expenditure exceeded its income by about 25 per cent and sales of assets helped to balance the books. In fact the Tories of the old Corporation were in for something of a surprise for Bristol went against the trend and sustained a Conservative majority in the new Council. Even Liverpool Council, the most predominantly Tory of Victorian urban authorities, experienced an interlude of Liberal control in the backlash against the unreformed system. Bristol, however, had a Conservative Council from 1836 until the Edwardian period, which is surprising when one considers the town's parliamentary history. Bristol was a solidly Liberal seat from 1852 through to 1885 and even before that, when political fortunes were more evenly balanced, there was only one post-reform election (1835) when the Tories captured both seats.

Why was there such a discrepancy between the town's municipal and Parliamentary elections? Admittedly, Bristol Conservatives benefited from the aldermanic system, which exaggerated even a small majority of elected seats. Thus in the first election the Liberals were only five seats behind the Conservatives, and in 1836 and 1837 were actually two ahead on the basis of the councillors elected. But, having gained a bare majority, the Conservatives secured their position by having nomination of the aldermen. Even so, other towns were sometimes able to cope with this disadvantage. In Bristol Liberals fought with a fundamental defect—a politically biased ward allocation of seats. In Birmingham there had been real gerrymandering in the drawing of ward boundaries;

in Bristol it was the relative ward representation which meant that Tories played the political game with heavily loaded dice.

It would have been wholly alien to contemporary Whig philosophy to have incorporated into municipal reform the principle of ward allocation in conformity with ratio of population. A uniform mathematical ratio of seats to population was no part of the 1832 Reform Act nor was it so in 1835. Indeed the revising barristers were instructed to take account of rateable values in drawing up ward boundaries and allocating seats. It was through this loophole that Bristol Conservatism was to receive favoured treatment. Hence in Bristol there was much continuity in politics and personnel between the unreformed and the reformed system. Nevertheless, the Liberals were sufficiently numerous and vocal to force on the Conservative majority the efficiency and economy that municipal reform had aimed to achieve. Despite electoral reverses the Liberals were well placed in positions of local influence and dominated two important bodies, the bench of magistrates and the Municipal Charity Trustees, both as a result of Whig government nomination. By paring expenditure and by further sales of corporate land, the municipal debt of £110,000 was cleared off by 1840, including outstanding compensation from the 1831 riots. After much bitter dispute with the Charity Trustees, the Council finally settled out of court, in 1842, by paying over funds which in some way recompensed the town's charities for earlier corporate misdemeanours. An efficient police force was set up and minor nuisances controlled. A modest commitment to improvement was made by the 1840 Improvement Act, concerned with street redevelopment. The inherited debt, together with an intrinsic caution, made Bristol Council a very conservative body that in its first decade acquired few new functions (Bush, 1976, 152-81).

Despite the fact that the Council was 'a steward rather than an innovator' it could not be indifferent to the interests of the town as had its predecessor. It was essentially a public rather than a private body and in time this drew the Council towards a greater concern for Bristol affairs and consequently a more important role in the town. This was clearly displayed in two important issues in the 1840s, the dock question and public health. The economic well-being of the town was tied to the Bristol docks, whose relative importance in trade had declined sharply largely because of a punitive rise in port dues levied by the Dock Company. Since the main indictment of the old Corporation had been its indifference to the fate of commerce in Bristol, it was likely that the reformed Council would display more concern. In 1839 the Council participated in plans for a revival of trade, which the directors of the Dock Company rejected. Thereafter municipalization of the docks was a serious possibility, and in 1840 the Council made an unsuccessful offer for the purchase of the company's shares. The scheme was revived in 1845 but it proved impossible to find a compromise on finance, and even arbitration terms could not be agreed. From 1846 the Council was being heavily pressed towards municipalization by the Free Port Association which became the most powerful local pressure group, and it was a mark of its achievement that every councillor elected in 1846 was committed to municipal ownership of the docks. Even an Admiralty enquiry confirmed that the only remedy for Bristol's decline was municipal control and a reduction of dock dues. In 1848 Parliament finally approved the transfer of ownership to the Council, which had spent £7,500 in securing the legislation, and which was now permitted to levy a 4d. rate to finance port administration. Substantial reductions in port dues were made, dock facilities were improved and perhaps coincidentally trade revived. Municipal reform had something to show by the 1850s and the functions of the Council were considerably extended by this resolution of the dock question.

A similar consequence flowed from the Council's commitment to public health. It was a great shock to Bristol opinion to see the town pilloried by the 1844–5 Health of Towns Commission, since Bristol was not an industrial city and it was assumed to be exempt from the sanitary evils of the north. Yet it had the third highest death rate (after Liverpool and Manchester) in England, and it lacked both public water supply and sewerage. The Council established a drainage committee, but until the passing of the 1848 Public Health Act responsibility ultimately lay with the Paving Commissioners of the old city. As elsewhere, the 'improvement' body resisted the extension of municipal control and argued forcibly, rather like the Birmingham Street Commission at about the same time, that public health in Bristol would be best served by a new more extensive act enlarging the functions of the Paving Commissioners. The Council faced this threat to its authority not with its own local act but with an appeal to the General Board of Health for a preliminary enquiry. The Board's inspector stressed the crucial lack of an effective authority in public health in Bristol and concluded, 'the grand defect and the parent of all others in the want of power on the part of the local government to interfere.' The Council was convinced, and it petitioned the General Board of Health for an order adopting the 1848 Act which would establish the Council as the local board of health. A fierce rearguard action ensued. The inspector's report was attacked as both erroneous and biased; the public was warned of the enormous costs which would flow from the new regime; the Paving Commissioners reiterated that they were the most appropriate body to supervise public health; and Joshua Toulmin Smith visited the town to preach the evils of centralization. All was to no avail, and in August 1851 Parliament designated Bristol Town Council as the agents of the 1848 Act.

During the next two decades the Council, by an energetic sanitary policy, put its cautious past firmly behind it. A measure of its achievement was that a death rate of 28 per thousand in 1850 had been cut to 22 in 1869, by which date Bristol was being cited for a sanitary regime which all authorities should emulate (Large and Round, 1974, 21-2). The most important task the sanitary committee undertook was the laying out of a main drainage and sewerage system for the whole city, and by 1866 Bristol had over one hundred miles of sewers. The regulation and inspection of privies, slaughterhouses and lodginghouses, the suppression of nuisances and the frequent cleansing of streets were all effectively undertaken. Bristol's water supply was considerably improved in the mid-Victorian period, though this was the work of the private water company which acted as an effective sanitary ally of the Council. Public health was always a slow plodding struggle, and sudden spectacular victories were rare, but Bristol could boast one when, as a result of a typhus epidemic, the Council belatedly agreed to the appointment in 1865 of a medical officer of health, Dr. David Davies. Davies was a keen supporter of a local medical authority, William Budd, who had worked on both cholera and typhoid and suggested a programme of preventative measures. Davies vigorously adopted Budd's ideas of isolation and disinfection, and the town reaped the rewards in its relatively low incidence of cholera and typhus, both of which threatened epidemics in Bristol in 1866. Budd proudly told the Royal Sanitary Commission in 1869 that 'the happy conditions of Bristol is merely an illustration of the condition into which the whole country might be brought if the local authorities exercised their functions properly.'

By the end of the 1860s the Council was being drawn towards greater involvement with the welfare of the community. The very commitment to public health bore the seeds of further responsibilities because of the ever-widening concept of what was needed to improve the health of the community. The Council was pushed in this direction in the late sixties and seventies by the growing number of new councillors, mostly Liberal Nonconformists, who were imbued with a belief in 'social citizenship' (Meller, 1976, 99–104). Like the 'civic gospel' advocates in Birmingham, these Bristol Liberals had been actively concerned in philanthropic, social and religious work, which had familiarized them with physical conditions and social needs in the city. There was no substitute for personal knowledge in initiating social action, and as a humble ratepayer had pointedly written in 1854, 'theres the cholera acoming and the stink under my windows is worse than ever . . . I should main like his worshipe the Mayor to come and smell it of a Sunday, if it dident do he good, perhaps twood the city for then he'd talk about it.' [sic][2] When wealthy families like the Frys and the Wills (of chocolate and tobacco fame) discovered the social conditions of the poor in their missionary work among the poor they were moved to urge on the Council more positive social role on behalf of all citizens. Like Canon Barnett, the pioneer social reformer from the East End of London who moved to Bristol in 1893, they were moved by a vision of an 'ideal city' in which the municipality would be responsible for the welfare of the urban community, providing for its economic, social and cultural needs.

So, in the last quarter of the century Bristol Town Council moved beyond sanitation as a first stage in improving the urban environment towards 'civilization'. The first public library run by the Council was opened in 1876, and other branch libraries soon followed. In 1887 Bristol, in common with many other cities, accepted the offer of a public park from a benefactor to mark the Jubilee of Queen Victoria. Generous benefactions in the 1890s provided a central library, museum and art gallery. In all these facets of new municipal administration private benefaction overcame financial stringency as the ratepayers faced the recurrent running costs but not the initial capital outlay. Perhaps the Council's policy on swimming baths best typefies the new attitude to local government. Initially in 1849 the Council had adopted the 1846 Baths and Washhouses Act solely as a public health measure, and even when first and second class swimming baths were opened in 1870 the motive was still primarily utilitarian, as swimming was traditionally regarded as the main means of cleansing. However, as domestic water supplies improved and swimming grew in popularity as a sport, so the sanitary had to give way to the recreational idea. In 1884 the proudest symbol of Bristol civic pride was opened: Jacob's Wells swimming baths, with their lavish architecture and the municipal coat of arms carved in stone. As it has recently been pointed out, this building 'remains as a living witness of the momentous change in attitude of the council towards it responsibilities . . . evidence that the council's response was more than a philanthropic gesture, it was a fulfilment of the ideal of "social citizenship".'[3] And the wealthy Liberal Nonconformist who persuaded the normally careful Bristol Council to embark on so extravagant a project rested his case firmly upon the duty of the local authority to protect the public health. In the 1840s that had meant protecting the community from environmentally sustained diseases; in the 1880s it meant caring for the health of the individual by providing for his recreational and cultural needs. In Bristol, as elsewhere, early Victorian local government was a matter of sewers and water, late Victorian of swimming baths, parks and libraries.

LEICESTER

In many respects, the unreformed Bristol Corporation was similar to that at Leicester. Both were venerable institutions with a long lineage and both were symbolic cynosures of local life. Yet whereas Bristol exhibited only some of the flaws of the old system of local government, Leicester personified all of them. Indeed the Webbs, having researched on most of the unreformed corporations, found Leicester the worst of the self-elected bodies. In earlier days the Corporation had established its reputation by defending the integrity of the borough of Leicester against the grasping colonialism of the county gentry: in more recent times it had seriously slipped from grace. In its last half century of existence the Leicester Corporation displayed the four cardinal defects of the whole unreformed system — political and religious exclusiveness, maladministration of charities, subservience to private interests and the perversion of public funds to politics (Greaves, 1939, 86). Little wonder that Leicester occupied so prominent a place in the story of municipal reform, for, in the words of one critic, the Corporation's 'foul and filthy corruptions have stunk in the nostrils of the whole nation.'

The political and religious exclusiveness of the Corporation in a town where radicalism and Dissent were growing rapidly was essentially the origin of the bitter party feuds which gripped Leicester in the half century prior to 1835. Solidly Tory-Anglican, the Corporation firmly set its course against any accommodation with the rising tide of Whig-radical nonconformity in the town. The Municipal Corporations Commission confirmed the all-pervading spirit of political partisanship which infused Leicester Corporation:

> In no corporation has a more complete system of political exclusiveness existed. . . . From the Mayor to the humblest servant

of the Corporation, every office has been filled by persons of the Corporation or Tory party, to the total exclusion of all who entertained different opinions, however wealthy, intelligent and respectable. . . . Diversity of religious faith has also formed an equal ground of exclusion . . . no Dissenter has ever been elected into the Corporation. . . . [which] produced in the minds of the excluded party a sense of grievance and injustice by which the vehemence of party spirit has been materially aggravated.[4]

One of the manifestations of this political exclusiveness was the gross partisanship in the administration of charities for which the Corporation was trustee. It was notorious that the Corporation distributed charity funds to its own supporters, and that it was futile for any Dissenter, however poor, to apply for financial help. Moreover this political distribution was only one facet of charity maladministration. Funds were mysteriously whittled away, often finding their way into corporate pockets, and the wishes of benefactors were often grossly distorted. Alderman Sir Thomas White's charity was set up to provide annual grants to 'humble tradesmen' to help them set up in business. By the early 1830s the humble recipients included 'ex-mayors, aldermen and common councilmen, surgeons, druggists, surveyors, hotel and innkeepers and first rate shopkeepers.'

When the Whig opposition attempted to probe charity matters, the Corporation deflected criticism with the assertion that private interests were not answerable to any public forum. Like many others, the Leicester Corporation was a major owner of property from which it derived a considerable income, and like them it regarded itself as a private body whose sovereignty could not be impugned. In 1822 a mayor asserted, 'the Corporation were possessed of considerable estates in their own proper right and over these estates had by law as free and ample a dominion as any individual over his own private property,' a view sustained by an ally who argued that corporate funds were 'their own to do as they like with as a body.'[5] Yet the Corporation's expenditure, partly financed from a borough rate, grew from £400 to £4,000 *per annum* in the early nineteenth century for the extremely limited public functions which the Corporation acknowledged. Even when in the 1820s the Corporation proposed to enlarge its improvement functions and to raise extra revenue for the goal, public distrust was so great that the necessary measures had to be dropped. Leicester was to remain a unique example of a corporate town with no improvement institution.

The grossest defect in Leicester was the Corporation's blatant use of its public functions and public funds for political purposes. Corporate dominance was manifested in the virtual nomination of two Tory M.P.s to sit for the borough. This was achieved through partisan creation of freemen, political manipulation of licences, especially to publicans, and simple bribery with corporate gold. Dissension within the Corporation, however, allowed Whig political fortunes to prosper and in 1818 and 1820 one Whig, Thomas Pares, was returned to Parliament. Finding its authority thus challenged, the Corporation resolved to correct the position and devote its whole energies to the re-assertion of corporate influence. The members pooled their collective knowledge and nominated 800 new freemen who were expected to vote Tory at the next election, one third of whom resided outside the county (Greaves, 1940).* The 1826 election, though hailed as a victory for the corporate interest, was indeed a Pyrrhic one. In pushing its endeavours to the limit, the Corporation had sold a hostage to fortune in three respects. First, it had participated in the grossest bribery, which undermined its moral position. Second, it had run up a huge debt which was to bear heavily upon it for the next decade. Third, and most important of all, it had planted a cuckoo in its own nest. The second Tory candidate, Otway Cave, not only refused to pay his share of the electoral expenses but also became the main anti-Corporation spokesman in Parliament and made embarrassing revelations about corporate corruption. Leicester

---

*Cf. J. Parkes to Lord Brougham 20 September 1833, 'in 1824–5 the Town Clerk was instructed by the corporators to send out circulars to 2000 foreign Tories, requesting them to take up their freedom with remission of fees — 800 accepted the offer . . . in 1826 these worthies spent £10,000 in the election . . . this sum they subsequently borrowed on their bond and now it remains a debt . . . of the Corporation estates.' Brougham Mss. (University College, London).

Corporation was thereby arraigned and convicted by public opinion long before 1835. Never can a corporation have paid so high a price to secure its political position.

Leicester became a national synonym for corporate corruption, and its protected position was increasingly offensive to local radical opinion. It was hardly surprising that when the Whig government introduced the Reform Bill, Leicester expected its first fruits to be municipal reform. Where Birmingham anticipated currency reform and Manchester free trade, Leicester looked to a reformed Parliament to answer one simple question: 'does the Corporation exist for the Town of Leicester or the Town of Leicester with its forty thousand inhabitants for the benefit of the Corporation?.' The arrival of the Municipal Commissioners in Leicester was the occasion for a single-handed rearguard action by Thomas Burbidge, the Town Clerk, who refused to comply with 'Star Chamber tyranny', and who declined to open the Corporation books or to produce required documents (Patterson, 1954, 202). The Commission put the worst interpretation upon the Corporation's secrecy and accepted virtually intact all the accusations of the opposition, although those relating to the administration of justice were highly doubtful.

The Corporation was convicted in national eyes of the gravest misdemeanours, and reform gave local opinion the opportunity to render a verdict upon the old elite. Conservatives contested all wards at the first election, and though they made every effort to dissociate themselves from the misdeeds of the Corporation they were inevitably tarred with the corporate brush and were overwhelmingly defeated. The new Council was composed of 52 Liberals and only 4 Conservatives, and within two years Conservatives were being advised to boycott municipal elections as a deliberate strategy:

> Let the radicals manage affairs a little while longer and the growing disgust of the inhabitants at the measures they adopt will do more to annihilate the faction than the return of any minority of conservatives however respectable in number and character.[6]

Neither the boycott nor the later participation in municipal politics allowed the Conservative cause to prosper, and Leicester Town Council was solidly Liberal for the rest of the century. On gaining power the Liberals elected a completely Liberal aldermanic bench, distributed corporate posts to their own supporters and elevated a succession of Dissenters, particularly Unitarians, to the mayoralty, which for the next forty years had no Tory occupant. Well might a critic conclude, 'it is not a change of system, it is a change of men.' Yet some felt that so profound a change in personnel presaged an earth-shattering change of municipal policy. Leicester's local government was the centre of the world as far as one hysterical Tory was concerned and he designated the change of regime as:

> the triumph of democratic and infidel principles . . . the prevalence of a new doctrine . . . the *Sovereignty of the People* — the spawn of the French Revolution . . . it is the victory of sectarianism and faction. . . . Then will republicanism and anarchy, profligacy and profaneness, Socinianism and infidelity have free course.[7]

The consequences of municipal reform in Leicester were less profound, partly because the deadening hand of the old Corporation pressed so heavily upon the new Council. The Council inherited three pressing financial burdens from the old Corporation, a borough debt of £27,000, a legal dispute over defalcations in charity funds and a compensation claim from Burbidge, the ex-town clerk. The two latter involved prolonged and expensive court cases which were not settled until 1846 and 1853. The first priority of the Council was to reduce the debt by sale of properties and economical administration, and so bold municipal ventures were out of the question. A leading radical, J. F. Winks, who ran a municipal journal in 1835-6, anticipated that the Council would embark on a wide ranging programme of local improvements, including new covered markets, public walks and gardens, playgrounds and swimming baths, and a new town hall. Nothing so ambitious could be contemplated until the 1840s.

By the mid-1840s the borough debt had been cleared, and the financial caution which had resulted in the abandonment of a proposed improvement bill in 1840–1 was being replaced by a more adventurous spirit. The Chadwick Report of 1842 and the Health of Towns Commission both identified Leicester's death rate of 30 per thousand as being due to defective drainage and so a sewerage scheme was increasingly regarded as a pressing necessity. At last, after a decade of retrenchment, the climate was ripe for the Council to demonstrate its superiority over the unreformed Corporation, for 'just as selfishness, sensuality and ignorance were the characteristics of the old body so should philanthropy, public spirit and enlightenment be the attributes of the new one . . . something more than mere counting house merit is required in municipal matters.'[8] Such favourable omens did not prevent the most profound schism in the Liberal party once a programme of sanitation and improvement was proposed in 1845. Leicester Liberalism split between the 'improvers' or 'expenders' led by William Biggs and the 'economists' led by Joseph Whetstone (Patterson, 1954, 340–3).

Following a campaign on drainage and town improvement by the *Leicester Chronicle* in 1843 and 1844, discussions took place on the Council in preparation for an improvement act. There was no real disagreement about Leicester's needs, which included sewerage, water supply, a new cemetary, improved markets and a new town hall. Dissension arose when William Biggs, leader with his brother John of local Liberalism, decided that sewerage, water supply and the cemetery could be left to a joint stock company being then promoted by Edwin Chadwick, while the Council should concentrate upon town improvements for which he drew up a £50,000 scheme. Whetstone, the chairman of the finance committee and a careful guardian of the public purse, did not believe the town could afford so ambitious a scheme and wished to give pride of place to sewerage, the need for which was clearly indicated by a severe bout of typhus early in 1846. The Council was sharply divided on this issue and it spilled over into other facets of public affairs in the town to produce a split which was not to heal fully for a quarter of a century.

So profound a rift did not occur in a vacuum and was itself a many sided development. It was a good example of the way a large and virtually irremovable Council majority was prone to fragmentation once the threat of a political opposition was removed. The schism reflected deeper political disagreements on the suffrage and on religion, for Biggs led the radicals and Whetstone the moderate Liberals. It was also a question of personalities. Whetstone was a cautious man who envisaged local improvement progressing slowly as the wealth of the town grew. Biggs was an ambitious political careerist, something of a brash agitator, who, no doubt like Chamberlain, saw a great reputation to be made out of municipal reform. As an unkind detractor noticed, Biggs 'did not care to meddle with the "dirty work" of Town Drainage. There was no glory to be gained in "washing sewers with cold water," laurels were only to be won by the builder of Town Halls.'[9] Drains were below ground but a new town hall was a monument to municipal achievement which all could see. Biggs commanded a majority and the Council approved his scheme, which met some public protest. When hostile memorials from ratepayers were summarily dismissed this raised the perennial question of whether Council or ratepayers were sovereign. Leicester was to have its 'magnificent "Brummagem" town hall' whether it wished it or not, in which case what role was left for the burgesses?

> They must not interfere with their local governors. They must give up the antiquated notion of petitioning against what they do not approve of. They must trust the benevolent despotism of the Town Council. They must patiently and confidingly wait until the good things that are in store for them are distributed among them. They must never think for a moment that they have any part to fulfil than that of submission.[10]

Such satirical jibes (similar to those provoked by a Liverpool Council hell bent on a water scheme that public opinion opposed) called into question the very nature of municipal reform. Yet beyond them lay the two features of the Leicester improvement dispute that are of most significance for the municipal historian. The controversy was at heart one of priorities. Then, as now; there were insufficient resources to finance all desirable municipal projects and so the Council was required to establish its order of priorities. The competing demands of sanitation and town improvement had to be resolved and for the Whetstone party the choice was clear. As one of them sourly told the poor 'Fever may enter your dwelling and strike to the earth your life's partner . . . or it may rob you of some of your little ones . . . what then? Have you not a great Market Place and a beautiful Town Hall to look at?'[11] Biggs believed that the sanitary needs of the town could be met by private capital and his vision of town improvement was a noble one. He wished, like the Medici of Florence, to elevate urban life through embellishment, and to emulate Caesar, 'who found Rome built of brick and left it built of marble.' Yet therein lay the dilemma — did the Council primarily exist for civic pride or sanitation? Whetstone opposed the joint stock company idea not just because of the practical difficulties but because it was abhorrent to him for the Council to shrug off what ought to have been its prime responsibility. Though the town could manage a little while longer with its deficient market arrangements and its outmoded town hall, it ought not to tolerate any longer its excessive mortality due to deficient drainage. The correct sequence appeared to be sanitation first and then civic pride, whereas Biggs seemed to reverse the order.

The second significant feature of the Leicester controversy concerns the terminology used to describe the parties, Biggs's 'expenders' and Whetstone's 'economists.' We have already seen how ratepayers' 'economist' groups were responsible for delaying the progress of municipal reform. The fear of increased rates was a perennial obstacle which any advocate of an extensive municipal policy had to overcome, and so the Leicester 'economists' fit into a familiar pattern. But Whetstone, though designated an 'economist', was Leicester's most consistent supporter of sanitary reform over the next two decades. In 1867 he was still preaching the languare of priorities, and he asked the Council 'would they indulge in the orgamental and leave the necessary undone?.' Whetstone was not against all municipal expenditure, but he opposed that which he did not deem to be of prime importance. Hence the term 'economist' is applied to two quite distinct features of municipal affairs. There was the negative parsimony which was intrinsically hostile to public expenditure and which James Hole in Leeds had identified, or which the government inspector Robert Rawlinson made famous in 1864:

> The popular local economist . . . generally ignorant of sanitary science. . . . thinks prevention is not better than cure; he has probably been born with a stupid head, a hard heart and a strong constitution; eats, drinks, breathes and exists; "stinks" he declares are wholesome and he instances night-men, tallow melters, butchers and ends up with 'Look at me, sir, stinks don't kill me.'[12]

The attitude of a Whetstone in Leicester or an Avery in Birmingham was wholly different. They opposed largesse and 'unnecessary' expenditure but they strongly advocated judicious and efficient expenditure on sanitation. Both, for instance, advocated municipal ownership of water supply. 'Economists' thus had both a negative and a positive public face.

The Leicester dispute had ended in a rather messy compromise, when Biggs dropped the new town hall and accepted a more modest improvement scheme. Public health provision was not supplied by the joint stock company which collapsed and the minimal sanitary administration of Leicester was provided under the Nuisance Removal Act of 1846, which the Council adopted. In October 1846 the Council agreed to pay modest fees to two medical officers who would certify the existence of nuisances. Their reports strengthened the case of those who, wishing to avoid the cost of a local act, argued for the adoption of the 1848 Public Health Act. In 1849 this was done, and the Town Council became the Local Board of Health, delegating its functions to the highways and sewerage committee, whose chairman was for many years Joseph Whetstone. In the next twenty-five years the Board of Health accounted for about a third of total borough expenditure which rose from £33,000 in 1850 to £158,000 in 1874. One of the Board's main activities, and a continuation of the nuisance removal of the late 1840s, was the field of building regulations. Leicester grew very rapidly in the third quarter of the century as its staple industry, the manufacture of hosiery, emerged from depression and as the town's economy diversified with the growth of the boot and shoe and engineering industries. (Plumb, 1958). Speculative building met the housing demand generated by a 40 per cent growth in population in the 1860s, which was accompanied by a running battle between the Board of Health, anxious to enforce building regulations and ingenious speculative builders seeking to avoid them. For instance, well intentioned building societies might lay out terraces with gardens only to find rows of cottages erected between the streets in the gardens themselves. Though the Board of Health did improve the standards of accommodation for the working class, it did not prevent some of the new suburbs becoming as insanitary as the ancient town. This has led to some disagreement in assessing the work of the Board. One researcher concluded that the Leicester Board of Health was a model of enterprising and enlightened local authority (Elliott, 1971, 181), whereas a recent general history of the town asserted that the Board 'was timid, unwilling to use its full powers to stop objectionable practices.' (Simmons, 1974, 10).

There was no comparable disagreement over the long term achievements in drainage and sewerage. In the early years the Board experienced at first hand the inhibiting restrictions of a centralized bureaucracy. Thomas Wicksteed was retained to design a sewerage system, and his scheme did not meet with Chadwick's approval. The town was then frustrated by pettyfogging criticisms from the General Board of Health:

> In vain does the Town Council persevere with a laudable wish to promote public health, in promoting a well-discussed, well matured, carefully constructed scheme—there is a power which stands above it in the metropolis which throws obstacles in its way . . . It is trifling with the commonweal of a large community . . . and that at a season when the mortality of the town is unprecedented.[13]

Eventually this was overcome and Wicksteed's scheme was completed in 1855, providing Leicester with its first drainage and sewerage scheme.

Having spent £45,000 upon sewerage, the Council was naturally reluctant to spend more, yet in time the deficiencies of the system had to be admitted as the town's population grew. In hot dry periods the stench from the river Soar was unbearable, and after heavy rain the river flooded and sewage flowed back into the system. The peculiarly high level of infant mortality in Leicester maintained the pressure for further sanitary reform, but it was only with the appointment of Joseph Gordon as borough surveyor in 1880 that the town recruited an engineer with the vision and imagination to go beyond remedial patching to the design of a completely new system. Between 1886 and 1890 Gordon's plans for a new system of main sewers for sewerage and flood prevention were implemented. The whole scheme cost £300,000 and rid the town of its historic hazards of flooding and filth. Soon afterwards a local antiquarian (Storey, 1895) described the project as 'outside the ordinary duties of local government . . . a monument of the courage and enterprise of the Council of Leicester,' a view echoed by the town's most recent historian (Simmons, 1974, 15) who wrote of 'a monument to the corporate pertinacity and patience of the Town Council.' The fruits of such municipal endeavour were soon gathered when the death rate fell below 15 per thousand in the early years of the twentieth century. Once more municipal reform justified itself through sanitary administration.

BRADFORD

Bradford was the fastest growing British city in the first half of the nineteenth century, increasing eightfold between the censuses of 1801 and 1851. Yet this rapid population explosion was contained within a local government structure that was little more than manorial. In the first four decades of the century the town relied heavily upon its parochial officers — constables, overseers, churchwardens and surveyors. The only concession to modernity and the facts of Bradford life was the Improvement Commission established in 1803, whose composition was renewed by co-option. Bradford was living witness of the fast developing specialization within the Yorkshire cloth industry. Specializing in the worsted trade, it was dubbed 'Worstedopolis' by a local antiquary (Cudworth, 1888). It was from the ranks of the worsted magnates, many of them radical Dissenters, especially Congregationalists, that the promoters of incorporation emerged. Though Bradford was enfranchised with two MPs in 1832, as an unincorporated town it was unaffected by municipal reform and no attempt to secure incorporation occurred until the mid-1840s. The incorporation movement grew out of a strong Liberal thrust which politicized Bradford's local institutions in the early-Victorian years. As in many early industrial towns the traditional Tory elite of Anglican merchants, professionals and gentry was being challenged by the newer families of recent migration or fortune whose religion and politics conflicted with the entrenched elite. Church rates, the Poor Law, the Improvement Commission and the Highways Board each became a battleground for this struggle within the Bradford bourgeoisie, and Liberals hoped to use both the political will which had captured local institutions and the political power of those bodies to sustain the case for incorporation.

The demand for incorporation centred on three main issues, each of which produced a counterblast from anti-incorporation groups. At the heart of the attempt to secure a charter for Bradford lay that same belief in representative institutions which imbued municipal reformers elsewhere. The possibilities for popular participation offered by the vestry in parochial appointments did not mitigate Liberal distaste for the self-elective constitution of the Improvement Commission, which was really Bradford's main local government agency. Bradford incorporators detested their closed Commission, as did their counterparts in Birmingham, and in the first town meeting on the Charter in 1843 a leading Liberal, George Oxley, argued that:

> A corporate body is superior to any other government . . . because it combines the purposes of improvement with the principle of liberty, and resting on the representative basis it acknowledges the vital principle of the British constitution that no

man shall be taxed without a voice in the choice of him who shall tax him.[14]

It was this principle which had led Cobden to argue that the 1835 Act was the most democratic ever enacted by Parliament, but it failed to win over Bradford's working-class radicals, who firmly allied with the Tory anti-incorporators. The Tory-radicals argued, with some justification, that Bradford Liberals 'for their own personal aggrandisement are very anxious to set up a new form of local government.' It was true that Bradford worthies, such as Henry Forbes, Robert Milligan and Titus Salt, wished to create an institution which would confirm their social leadership in the town. Here was the 'tyranny of the bloated rich' again, and in 1850 a Tory critic recalled Liberal motives, 'violent political changes had not given them all the patronage which profit and pride had hoped for. A Corporation offered an easy means of placing everything in their grasp.'

This political motivation, whether high-principled or selfishly expedient, was firmly linked to a second issue—law and order. As a recent researcher (Elliott, 1976, 24) has explained, 'Bradford was a rough town in every sense of the word . . . it resembled a frontier town in the American West or Australia in the 1870s.' Riots were not uncommon; some, like that in 1837 against the imposition of the new Poor Law, were quite serious. In addition there seemed to contemporaries an abnormally high degree of theft, brawling, drunkenness and prostitution. One of the great advantages of a corporation would be that it would establish an efficient police force to protect the property and reform the morals of the citizenry. As in Manchester in the previous decade, the imposition of an authoritarian police force was an extremely sensitive issue for working-class radicals and chartists, and Squire Auty, leader of the Bradford operative Conservatives (working-class Tories), did not hesitate to exploit fear of the police as a political weapon. It was widely acknowledged that crime and immorality were partly the product of urban squalor, and concern for sanitary improvement was the third plank in the incorporation propaganda war. Lack of drainage and sewerage, pollution of the becks, the erection of overcrowded and insanitary slums, and the appalling smoke nuisance were all cited as compelling reasons for a charter. The logic flowed from a widespread dissatisfaction with the Improvement Commission, whose powers and area of jurisdiction were insufficient to cope with the problems. Here, however, an interesting counter-proposal was made. Rather than accept the compelling logic of municipal reform, Tories wished to preserve and enhance the position of the Commission by the promotion of an improvement act which would endow the commissioners with new powers to deal with sanitation. The Tory-radical alliance against incorporation was cemented by the creation in 1845 of a Sanitary Committee, comprising representatives of the Woolcombers' Committee (established to collect evidence on the poverty of the woolcombers) and prominent Tory-Anglican philanthropists. As the woolcombers pointed out, the middle class had the opportunity to improve both the monetary and the physical condition of the town, first by improving wage rates and secondly by cleaning up the mess which rapid industrialization had occasioned. Anti-incorporators sourly pointed out that the Liberal capitalists had taken the profits of economic growth but expected the community of ratepayers to bear the costs.

The incorporation party did not have things their own way during the campaign and their opponents were able to convince the Privy Council that a charter should not be granted. The charter petition received 10,800 signatures, the counter petition 12,200. After a scrutiny the Privy Council inspector reduced these to 8,700 and 10,700, and, crucially, calculated that those against a charter represented a rateable value of £96,000, while those in favour only £78,000. The petition was therefore denied in August 1845, but Bradford was assured by a neighbouring protagonist that the lack of a corporation was no bar to social progress:

> Corporations as now constituted are neither certain nor the only instruments of practical benefit. They are more frequently, like a bone of contention, a subject of political excitement and perennial agitation, a state of things but little conducive to either moral or physical improvement.[15]

The Commissioners' improvement act, which appeared perhaps the best that could be hoped for, did not in fact materialize, since in 1846 the incorporation campaign was renewed, quietly and more effectively. Liberals were in tune with the Russell ministry and, no doubt through Lord Morpeth, M.P. for the West Riding and a government minister, were able to prepare the ground for a second application. In April 1847 the charter was granted and the first municipal election took place in August.

As elsewhere, municipal reform was a triumph for the Liberals. Disconsolate Conservatives toyed with the idea of a boycott of the elections, a move roundly criticized by one of their number:

> I feel there is much apathy and indifference existing among Conservative Gentlemen of the Borough as to their desire to form part of the Council. It would have been a useless expense to convene a counter petition . . . [but] it would ill-behove such of you as are Conservative to stand aloof and neglect the best interests of your fellow-townsmen.[16]

In fact Conservatives gained a quarter of the seats in August 1847 and increased this to over a third in November. This could not, of course, prevent the Liberals from choosing their own aldermen and mayor. Magnanimously allowing the Conservatives one aldermanic seat, the Liberals began the first full year of Bradford's municipal history with a 40–16 advantage. Robert Milligan was elected mayor, J. A. Cooper, town Clerk, and a predominantly Liberal bench of magistrates nominated. It was a triumph for the political and social aspirations of the Liberal, Nonconformist millocracy (Cudworth, 1881).

As opponents of the charter had warned, the mere fact of incorporation did little to mitigate the sanitary evils which, it had been argued, made the creation of a Town Council a pressing necessity. In 1848 the Council was able to introduce by-laws against minor nuisances, including the quaint regulation, aimed at protecting public morality, forbidding women to clean windows more than six feet off the ground. Any more fundamental attack upon the sanitary state of

Bradford required the passage of a separate improvement bill, even though the Council now acted as improvement commissioners by the terms of the charter. As if to confirm the Council's lack of powers, the town suffered a major visitation of cholera in the summer of 1849. This spurred the Liberals into action and a group of leading Council members, with the help of the town clerk, drafted an improvement bill for submission to Parliament. The Bradford Improvement Act of 1850 proved as contentious a political issue as the charter itself. All those who had opposed the charter now fought a second battle against the Liberal majority. It was argued that there would be increased rates, huge borough debts, the subservience of the out-townships to the needs of Bradford's central and insalubrious districts and the creation of a network of jobbery and nepotism. The principle of town improvement must always be related to the facts of political life, and in Bradford in 1850 enhanced municipal authority meant increased Liberal power and patronage. The charter had merged the Improvement Commission with the Council, and now three years later the Highway Surveyors were to be swallowed. In the summer of 1850 public affairs in Bradford became extremely acrimonious owing to the devious means by which the bill was being promoted. In order to prevent both Council debates and ratepayers' meetings the legislation was put forward as a private bill from a small group of Liberals acting in their private and not their public capacity. The Council petitioned in favour of the bill, but it was not a Council bill as such.

In the event parliament, and not local opposition, determined the outcome. A number of clauses were dropped, notably those relating to water supply and cemeteries, and it was insisted that a large part of the 1848 Public Health Act be incorporated with the bill. This was the price Bradford had to pay to get its bill enacted, and it left the town in an intermediate position between places such as Leeds and Liverpool, which had their own acts, and Leicester or Bristol which had adopted the 1848 Act. Bradford had not adopted the 1848 Public Health Act, though it was subject to some General Board of Health supervision (mainly financial) because the 1850 Bradford Improvement Act incorporated part of the general act. There was no preliminary enquiry such as occurred when the 1848 Act was provisionally adopted, and Bradford was under direct central control only when it required authority to raise loans. This occurred in 1851 when the Council, as Local Board of Health, wished to embark on a major street improvement scheme. Robert Rawlinson inspected the town to verify that the redevelopment programme was needed, and the General Board tartly explained that no such enquiry would have been necessary had the 1848 Act been fully adopted and a preliminary enquiry held. In fact Rawlinson not only reported on the street improvement scheme, he also commented on the general state of the town, confirming the need for major sanitary reform. He noticed:

> Defective street pavements, confined courts, contaminated open water-courses, crowded cellar dwellings, unregulated common lodging houses, open and closed privies and middens crowded upon dwelling-houses and under them with large spaces unoccupied and unenclosed covered with refuse and filth so as to form a nuisance to the whole neighbourhood . . . the slaughterhouses are confined and crowded in amongst houses and warehouse property.[17]

Though Rawlinson's report ruffled some local feathers, in fact the Bradford Town Council was quite willing to take technical, financial and legal advice from the General Board of Health. When in difficulties with the surveyor appointed to plan the sewerage scheme, the Council was relieved to accept assistance from a General Board inspector who shared in the planning and supervision of the scheme. Indeed the Council was anxious to use the Board's authority and advice to resist political opponents locally. In the event Bradford welcomed the degree of centralization to which it was subject, for in practice it was free to go its own way but to use the General Board as the occasion demanded.

By far the most important municipal achievement in the Council's early years was the corporation purchase of the waterworks in 1854 (Elliott, 1976, Chap. 6). In the original proposals for the 1850 Improvement Act there had been plans for an eventual municipal purchase of the water company but the relevant clauses had been dropped. The town was alerted to the problems of water supply by the hot summer of 1852 when supplies were interrupted. When the Bradford Waterworks Company announced its intention to build new reservoirs the Council decided to contest the issue and seek full municipal control. There followed a two year battle of intense ferocity between the company and the Council centring on environmental, legal, financial and technical issues. Underlying all the complex factual disputes lay an ideological debate about social utilities. Private companies, however altruistic, were essentially concerned with making a profit: public waterworks were essentially concerned with serving the local community. This conflict between public and private interests ran through the whole waterworks dispute, for, as one correspondent explained:

> The Corporation, being a public body, cannot be supposed to be actuated by sordid motives of gain to their own individual purses but having solemn obligations to perform towards their citizens, they may at times come into collision with what are supposed to be the interests of private individuals and companies of shareholders.[18]

The Bradford water issue was complicated, first by the fact that the neighbouring town of Keighley opposed the scheme and second because a wealthy dyer, H. W. Ripley (M.P. for the borough 1874–80), attempted to provide the town with a water supply himself, and began laying pipes in private streets. A very expensive contest ended ignominiously when Parliament rejected both the Council's and the company's schemes in 1853.

The immediate aftermath of the frustration of the Council's plans was indeed demoralizing for municipal reformers. The courts refused to grant an injunction restraining Ripley's employees laying water pipes, and then issued one against the Council to prevent the £8,000 expenses of the 1853 Parliamentary application being charged to the rates. On the one hand the Council's authority in its own streets had been flouted, and on the other municipal reformers faced the prospect of paying large expenses out of their own pockets.

Joseph Farrar, one of the leading advocates of full municipal ownership, was temporarily diverted from the collectivist path by this financial threat. Ultimately it was public opinion which sustained frail hearts, for the 1853 municipal elections, which were fought solely on the water question, were a resounding victory for those who favoured municipal ownership. Armed with popular support the Council renewed its application and forestalled a further battle with the company by agreeing terms for the purchase beforehand and by adopting the company's scheme and its engineer. By the Bradford Waterworks Acts of 1854 the Council was empowered to buy up the company and construct reservoirs for the better supply of the town at a total cost of £240,000. Water from the Wharfe first reached Bradford in 1860, and the first reservoir remote from the town at Grimwith on the river Dibb, was completed in 1864. The improved water supply was of both practical and symbolic importance for the Council and the town. Municipalization of water supply was one of the main factors identified by the town clerk in 1859, when he told the National Association for the Promotion of Social Science annual meeting in Bradford that the death rate had fallen from 28 to 22 per thousand over the previous decade. 'The primary cause of this was the sanitary action of the Corporation,' he said, and cited scavenging, sewerage, new building regulations, supervision of lodging houses and suppression of cellar dwellings, in addition to municipal water supply. Whether the results were as yet so startling as he claimed may be doubted yet already the symbolic importance of a public water supply was clear. By this action the Council committed itself to a positive and collectivist role and this had been anticipated at the very outset when in August 1852 a Bradford councillor had foretold that:

> When the Town Council possessed these works instead of looking for a revenue beyond what would maintain the works in efficiency, their chief object would be to make the works instrumental to the promotion of the cleanliness and the comfort of all classes of citizens.[19]

Municipal concern for cleanliness and comfort of the community would in time take Bradford towards the muncipal socialism of the late nineteenth and early twentieth centuries.

SHEFFIELD

Sheffield, with which Bradford is sometimes compared, had a much cloudier municipal history. Like Bradford's, its first application for a charter was rejected. In 1838 leading members of the Sheffield Reform Association organized an incorporation petition which met with strong Tory-radical opposition. There was powerful local resistance to the new Poor Law and the prolific anti-Poor Law pamphleteer, Samuel Roberts, turned his vitriolic pen against the idea of incorporation. In a town with a very egalitarian political tradition, which flowed from its even social structure, the notion of an official elite was antipathetic, and at the outset one radical ominously warned, 'by means of a corporation you will be raising up an aristocracy among you and also creating a set of masters over you.' The opponents of a charter gained 15,300 signatures while the proposers obtained only 9,600. After scrutiny the proposers were reduced to a mere 1970 and the opponents to 4,589, with the rateable values at £46,000 and £77,000. The application was denied and was not to be renewed for a further five years. When the incorporation idea was revived it was as a result of moves by the county bench of magistrates attempting to control the police in the borough. One of the great aims of Richard Cobden in seeking the incorporation of Manchester had been to release the town from landed control, and similarly Sheffield's leading citizens represented the assumption that it was no more than a village community. In August 1843 a charter was granted and the first elections were held in November. The Sheffield Town Council, largely ruled by its iron and steel magnates, was at first a very hesitant body, constrained by lack of powers and rival local institutions, the Improvement Commission, the Highway Boards and the Town Trustees (Walton, 1948, 183–5).

Apart from the establishment of a borough police force

there were few obvious signs that the Council had been born, for it was not until 1848 that even a commission of borough magistrates was appointed. Council affairs were enlivened in the later 1840s by the infusion of a substantial number of Chartist councillors who with other local radicals formed the so-called Sheffield Democrat party. In 1849 Chartists filled eight of the fourteen vacancies in the November elections and commanded twenty-two of the Council's forty-six seats (Pollard, 1959). One of these ultra-radicals was an eloquent and ambitious accountant, Isaac Ironside, who had entered the Council at a by-election in 1846 in Eccleshall, and was re-elected in 1847 and 1850. Concerned about all aspects of working-class welfare, Ironside succeeded in persuading the Council to appoint a health committee, whose first task was to commission a sanitary survey of the town (Salt, 1971). This sanitary report of 1848, by two local doctors, was arguably the first socially useful achievement of the Council, since it clearly demonstrated what was needed in Sheffield to improve environmental conditions:

> Better constructed dwellings, both as regards light and ventilation, and a better supply of water; the substitution of water closets for the present open privies . . . more spacious and commodious yards, well paved and drained, with public washhouses and baths in populous districts; and above all places for proper and rational recreation.[20]

It was to be many years before the Council was empowered to create such an environment and the process by which Sheffield Town Council became a potentially useful social institution took sixteen years to mature and may be likened to a three-act play.

The first part of the drama began in the ward organization of the Sheffield Democrats in the late 1840s and early 1850s. Under Ironside's leadership the radicals formed ward committees to organize municipal business, vetting candidates, originating motions and on one celebrated occasion even nominating aldermen. This was no less than a miniature caucus, and in language that was to become familiar in the 1870s, one critic complained of the Democrat movement, 'it has aimed to set up a dictatorship, armed with a set of organised cliques called "central democratic associations" . . . it has endeavoured to engross all local offices in the hands of subservient nominees of the moving power.'[21] Yet there was more to Ironside's organization than mere place-seeking, for he was promoting what his biographer has called 'experiments in anarchism' (Salt, 1972). Ironside converted the ward organization into a system of ward and township democratic self-government. Inspired by Joshua Toulmin Smith, the great anti-centralization propagandist, Ironside set up so-called 'ward-motes', small localized forums, conforming to Toulmin Smith's historical description of 'regular fixed frequent and accessible meetings . . . at which all matters . . . shall be laid before the folk and the people, discussed and approved or disapproved.'[22] It was, in short, a system of ward and township autonomy to rival the precept of municipal reform. With their own newspaper, the *Sheffield Free Press*, and with an indefatigable leader, Ironside, who told his followers that public business made such inroads into his domestic comfort that he had no time for personal friendships, the Sheffield Democrats were well placed to dominate municipal affairs. Indeed they even proposed their great prophet, Toulmin Smith, as an unsuccessful candidate for Liberal nomination for the Parliamentary election of 1852.

Given Toulmin Smith's views on the 1848 Public Health Act, and Ironside's advocacy of them in Sheffield, it was hardly surprising that any suggestions to adopt the 1848 Act would receive little support. The Council's motion on the Chadwickian Act was predictable:

> Undoubtedly it contains many excellent provisions suitable to the exigencies of this and other large towns, but the controlling power which it gives to the General Board of Health over some of the most important acts which local boards have to perform, and the distrust which it manifests as to their capacity or integrity to carry its provisions into proper effect, are alike objectionable and offensive and opposed to those principles of free local self-government, so congenial to the spirit and feelings of Englishmen.[23]

However, Ironside was deeply committed to sanitary reform and he supported the idea of an improvement act to be negotiated between the Council and a committee of ratepayers. The 1851 Sheffield Improvement Bill presaged a much more active and useful municipal future, and it was a notable symbolic moment in September 1851 when the leading 'aristocratic' Whig, Alderman Thomas Dunn, proposed and the leading Democrat, Isaac Ironside, seconded the motion to apply for parliamentary approval for the local act. By the end of the year this alliance was shattered as Ironside put his authority behind moves to delay the legislation which in effect killed the bill. Popular fears over taxation and arbitrary police powers, said Ironside, would have to be allayed by town meetings scrutinizing every clause in the bill. In fact the truth was that, having created township democracy, Ironside did not wish to see it supplanted by municipal authority and he later admitted that his main ground of opposition to the 1851 Improvement Bill was that it 'disfranchised a large number of ratepayers without the property qualification by abolishing the popular and simply elected highway boards and transferring their powers to the Town Council.'[24]

Ratepayer democracy would be ensured not by an enhanced town council but by preserved vestry institutions, and in the early 1850s Ironside's power base lay not in the Council but in the Sheffield Board of Highway Surveyors. Armed with only vestry authority Ironside used the Highways Boards to embark on a programme of sanitary reform, a project the Council had been prevented from launching. The contrast between an energetic Highways Board and an effete Town Council was truly remarkable. In the spring of 1852 Council expenditure was so low that there was no need to levy a borough rate, and in the summer of 1853 the Council assembled to find not a single notice on the agenda paper. Yet at the very same period the Board was quite illegally laying deep sewers in Sheffield streets. In advocating vestry and township autonomy and citing Toulmin Smith as his legal authority, Ironside was, interestingly, pursuing just that course of action which the great pundit had denounced in Birmingham in 1849. Then

Toulmin Smith had strongly argued for one all-powerful sanitary authority which had to be the Town Council.

There was always a strong streak of vanity in Ironside, and in time he over-reached himself. He offended many of his own party by his highhandedness, for he loved the role of petty dictator too well. Moreover he had established his own gas company which also operated without parliamentary approval, and eventually the courts firmly scotched his theory that ward-mote and vestry consent was sufficient to authorize any public action. The status of the Highways Board was much reduced when it was restored within its proper empire, and both in 1853 and 1854 Ironside was defeated in municipal elections. He was not to return to the Council until 1862, being re-elected again in 1865 (Furness, 1893, 35). Act One of the Sheffield municipal drama ended in the mid-1850s with the collapse of the Ironside empire.

The second act opened in the later 1850s with growing discontent about the unsatisfactory state of municipal affairs. The town was grateful to Ironside for his sanitary reforms, but it could not forever have unofficial and illegal government. Even since 1851 there had been spectacular growth with virtually new towns being set up in the suburbs, and no straining of legal powers would be sufficient to meet the needs of such a burgeoning population. In March 1858, therefore, the Council resolved to introduce an improvement bill, this time shorn of the powers of gas and water purchase which had caused some opposition in 1851. The subsequent six months witnessed an opposition to the bill far less disingenuous than in 1851. There were one major and three minor planks in the opposition case. The first minor issue was the old bugbear of taxation. The bill proposed to take over the powers of the improvement commission and the six Highway Boards in the borough and to consolidate all powers of taxation. There was to be a reduction in the power of taxation and a redistribution of it, but this did not prevent a great clamour against the supposed increased taxation in the bill. The second issue was the Leicester question of sanitation versus embellishment. The main force of the bill's provisions was towards sanitary reform, but there were also proposals for the building of a new town hall. The opposition propagandists were thus able to 'raise the hue and cry that it contemplates only a needless and outrageous expenditure, crushing the poor and driving them from their cottages that the town may be adorned with costly and splendid town halls.'[25] The third bone of contention was largely a tactical one and opponents of the Sheffield bill enquired whether it would not be better to adopt the newly enacted 1858 Local Government Act. This was rather specious since the anti-improvers really wanted neither the general nor the local act. Robert Leader, editor of the *Independent* and a persistent advocate of municipal reform, ably demonstrated the superiority of Sheffield's own measure:

> The Local Government Act is a general measure framed to apply . . . to all towns. It knows no local peculiarities. The Local Improvement Bill has been very carefully framed to meet not only the general but the special requirements of Sheffield. The difference between the two is just like that of buying a coat ready made and having a coat made to order. . . . The first is made very wide . . . the other is made to fit closely but easily.[26]

The claims of taxation, embellishment and general legislation were really no more than side shows. The main attraction was undoubtedly the issue of township autonomy. The crucial element in the 1858 struggle was that the Highway Boards were implacably opposed to the bill. Ironside was no longer on the Council but he still exercised great influence in the townships. He argued that the bill was unnecessary since the Highway Boards were effectively draining the town. The report adopted in June 1858 by the Sheffield Highway Board spoke for all the township institutions:

> The bill will do away with time-honoured vestries where the ratepayers have complete and effective control over the yearly expenditure and will enlarge the powers of the corporation, which body, to a considerable extent, is beyond the control and supervision of the burgesses.[27]

The Sheffield Improvement Bill of 1858 occasioned a fundamental conflict between ratepayer democracy and the municipal leviathan.

In an attempt to meet the opposition case, the bill's sponsor,

Alderman Dunn, proposed that a committee be appointed to suggest changes in the bill. One improver, fearing a sell-out, complained that this bill would be 'the second child that had been stabbed and buried by its own parents.' In fact the Council remained firm in its resolve to take over the township bodies, though it did agree to some other changes. The opposition rejected the compromise and directed its campaign towards the 1858 municipal elections, which would decide the fate of the bill. With marvellous disingenuousness the Ironside party organized meetings in every ward to refuse to support any candidate who favoured the bill, yet introduced a motion in the Council to refuse to receive ratepayers' memorials in support of the bill 'on the ground that they contain threats to those councillors or candidates who are opposed to the bill and that it is an attempt at coercion.'[28] Robert Leader powerfully stressed that the bill's object was that 'the abodes of the poor may be freed from those causes of disease from which the middle classes have escaped' but he warned his readers that on the first of November 'humbug' might have its day of triumph. So it turned out. In a formidable show of popular resistance every ward returned an opponent of the Improvement Bill in the 1858 elections. Though Ironside himself did not stand, the result was a great victory for his brand of community politics and his respectable anarchism. The second act of the drama ended in total gloom for municipal reformers when the bill was abandoned.

The third and final act began as inauspiciously as the second had ended. In 1859 the Registrar General had drawn attention to high mortality in Sheffield and this might have been the shot in the arm the town needed. The Council did not respond positively, and indeed in the following year decided 'it is not expedient at the present time to consider the most efficient means for improving the sanitary condition of the borough.' The Council, still under the sway of the 1858 anti-improvers, was not prepared even to 'consider' the question of sanitary reform. Council inertia accompanied continued population growth and at the 1861 census Sheffield exceeded 185,000 in population. It did seem incongruous that so large a town should still be without the means of effective local government, and as one reformer put it 'we cannot always be behind-hand in the race of improvement.' In 1864 the quest for improvement was renewed once more with the appointment in February of a Council committee to enquire into the possible adoption of the 1858 Local Government Act. In May the committee reported back to the Council in the most unequivocal terms:

> The adoption of the Act will make the Council what in principle it is, and what in practice it ought to be — the chief authority within the borough for all purposes of local government, uncontrolled except by the power of public opinion. . . . The powers of the Act are such as are required for improving the sanitary condition of the borough, for extending the accommodation which the increasing manufactures and commerce of the district call for and for carrying out those improvements which our wealth and intelligence demand.[29]

After a heated debate when one of the 1858 anti-improvers, now an alderman, argued that adoption of the report was conditional upon town meetings, the Council agreed to adopt the 1858 Act by a vote of 25 to 15.

The early summer passed with ominous signs of renewed opposition. As Alderman T. E. Mycock, for twenty years the chairman of the watch committee and a prominent Poor Law activist, had predicted, opposition came from 'the little coteries who composed the highway boards and who dreaded the loss of their little authority.' Town meetings were held hostile to the 1858 Act. When in 1858 the Council proposed a local act, the opposition had advocated a general act: now in 1864 the opposition called for a local act. It was an open question whether the Council's nerve would hold in the face of public criticism. There was one favourable condition. The town was rivetted upon the water question following the appalling disaster of the bursting of Dale Dike dam, which killed over 200 people. It was the possibility of municipal control of water supply (which did not in fact materialize until 1887) that was the central issue in Sheffield affairs in the summer of 1864 and this to some extent took the limelight away from the public health issue. In any event, the Council resisted township autonomy and confirmed its decision in July by a bigger majority 36 to 14. Municipal reformers were elated partly because at last the sanitary improvement of the town could begin, and partly because the rehabilitation of the Council itself was now possible. Lack of functions had made Council membership unattractive to the town's business elite. The creation of a politically useful role was a precondition to the establishment of the Council's social authority:

> The main reason for the degradation of the Council has been that the intellect and property of the town has stood aloof from it. The people have been taught that there was no one so ignorant or incompetent but he might become a town councillor. . . . The Town Council has had no self respect. Its powers were small. Its capacity was smaller. Yesterday the first step upward was made. . . . There is now time for the men of intelligence and public spirit to lay their heads together and devise the means of making the Town Council equal to the new demands upon it.[30]

In September 1864 the Town Council met for the first time as the local Board of Health. It thanked the Improvement Commission and the six Highway Boards (which were now amalgamated in the Council) for their services to the town. Even now there was an echo of former dissension, for a prior meeting of councillors had declined to include Ironside or his aldermanic lieutenant on the list of committees. When the nominations were proposed Ironside and his colleague walked out of the chamber, which was taken as a great insult to the mayor. The committees of the Board of Health began working but there were still the November elections to come. The trouncing of the improvement party in 1858 and the consequent lowering of the social quality of town councillors was well remembered. A victory for the remnants of the Ironside anti-improvement party would certainly prevent the effective implementation of the powers adopted under the 1858 Act. Though there was much talk, in the event only three of the nine wards were contested in the 1864 elections, which was less than normal (in the first quarter century of the Council's history over half the wards were contested). The improvers resisted the minor challenge that materialized and the work of sanitary and social improvement could begin.

It was only a beginning, and seven years later the town's

radical M.P., A. J. Mundella, could see little sign of civic duty or achievement. He told Leader:

> I see a pretty state of things in your municipality. Everything is mean, petty and narrow in the extreme. . . . Sheffield would do well to spend half a million in improvements. A better Town Hall might be followed by better Town Councillors, and more public spirit. . . . I wish you would preach the duty of the wealthy intellects of Sheffield taking their share in the elevation of the town.[31]

It was clear that after so inauspicious a municipal apprenticeship Sheffield was as much in need of the civic gospel as Birmingham.

Six

Municipal Authority in Victorian Cities

THE 1835 REVOLUTION

1835 has been hailed as one of the great turning points in modern English history—a veritable municipal revolution, in the Webbs' phrase. Yet, as we saw in earlier chapters, the system did not change very much, though the personnel did. In 1888, after the County Councils Act, the reverse happened. Though the expulsion from county government of its former leaders was widely predicted, it did not occur: but the system changed fundamentally. 1835 saw a change of men, while 1888 saw a change of system.

Perhaps then the Webbs got it wrong, and perhaps 1835 was not a municipal revolution. Perhaps indeed they were wrong to conclude their great history of English local government with the Municipal Corporations Act. Of course two important features of 1835 would support the idea of a municipal revolution. There was a most profound change in almost all of the 178 boroughs in the Act whereby those previously excluded from local government became its masters. Bristol was a rare example of a council that remained politically loyal to its predecessor, and Liverpool followed suit within a few years. But the great majority changed political colour overnight and this did wreak havoc in the channels of local political authority. For instance, a magistrate of thirty years standing who had been an alderman for decades and had several times been mayor naturally found it galling that he was no longer in the council nor on the bench in Russell's new commissions of J.P.s. No amount of qualification would convince such a man that in his local hemisphere a very real revolution had not taken place, that, in the words of one reformer, 'an extraordinary degree of power has been conferred upon a class previously thought undeserving of it — an immense change has taken place in the hands of those who exercise power.'[1]

The second revolutionary aspect of 1835 was that it contained the seeds of its own extension, an in-built potential for future momentum. The 1835 Act (as amended in 1837) established a procedure which, though under a legal cloud until the early 1840s, enabled non-municipal boroughs to gain a charter of incorporation. Hence, while it would be wrong to say that 1835 established an elected form of urban government, 1835 did designate the conditions by which such a system of local government could be created. To the original 178 municipal boroughs were soon added the urban industrial centres of the new society. Within two decades of the first municipal elections the following had gained charters (Vine, 1879, 60–2):

Ashton Under Lyne	1847
Birmingham	1838
Blackburn	1851
Bolton	1838
Bradford	1847
Brighton	1854
Devonport	1837
Hartlepool	1850
Honiton	1846
Manchester	1838
Middlesbrough	1852
Oldham	1849
Rochdale	1856
Salford	1844
Sheffield	1843
South Shields	1850
Stalybridge	1856
Tynemouth	1849
Wakefield	1848
Warrington	1847
Wolverhampton	1848
Yeovil	1854

Only four of this list were not industrial cities of the midlands and north, and so 1835 made possible the erection of local government institutions in towns of novel and rapid growth. And the process continued steadily through the century. By the late 1870s over 60 new boroughs had been incorporated, and in 1877 an act was passed which allowed the expenses of an incorporation petition to be charged to the rates (previously the petitioners as private citizens had had to bear the costs). In the last two decades a more rapid rate of applications was evident and by the turn of the century there were 313 municipal boroughs. Hence 1835 played its part in the adjustment of English political institutions to reflect the fact of a changed society.

Yet the true municipal revolution of the nineteenth century involved not the extension of the principles of 1835 but their transformation. The English municipal revolution occurred in the half century from 1835 when merely elementary representative institutions were transformed into powerful agencies with wide social purposes.

THE MUNICIPALIZATION OF LOCAL GOVERNMENT

There were two processes remodelling local government in nineteenth-century England. The first involved national legislation, initially permissive and later compulsory, which created a new system of local government and culminated in the two crucial acts of 1888 and 1894, discussed below. This was by and large a consciously planned, though not always logical, administrative process. Conversely, the development of urban government in corporate towns, which was the second process, sprang from no overall plan but was a response to local government problems as they were perceived in the local context. The transformation of municipal government between 1835 and 1900 was achieved primarily by local legislation promoted by local initiative. The fundamentally different nature of the two processes does not mean that the two were unrelated, for the eventual pattern of national legislation owed much to the success of private bill legislation on which corporate towns relied. The national adoption of the 'principles of 1835' occurred because of what the towns had made of them.

In the general development of local government based upon national legislation in the sixty years from 1834 three features may be discerned (Lipman, 1949, 34). First, there was a persistent tendency to create *ad hoc* bodies for particular services and later to absorb them into larger authorities. The second was the gradual transfer of power from smaller to larger units. And the third was the confirmation of the 'island' principle, that urban communities were to be treated as enclaves within a county, a principle that was enshrined in the 1888 County Councils Act. Within the 1834–1894 period the early 1870s were something of a watershed. Before then a multiplicity of agencies were created on the principle of administrative specialization: after that a search began for a more uniform and coherent local government system.

The reform of the Poor Law in 1834 set England on the road of administrative specialization, which was to cause so much confusion later in the century. Throughout the nineteenth century, and indeed right up to 1929, poor relief was administered by boards of Poor Law guardians directly elected by ratepayers. When we talk of all-powerful town councils developing by the end of the century we should not forget that poor relief always remained outside municipal control. The seminal 1834 Poor Law Amendment Act designated a Poor Law union as the administrative unit for poor relief which was to be created by amalgamation of parishes. By mid-century some 15,000 parishes in England and Wales had been reduced to about 600 unions supervised by a central authority, the Poor Law Commission (from 1847 the Poor Law Board). Union boundaries were, on the whole, drawn with some geographical sense but they often cut across historic county, borough and parish boundaries.

In 1835 Parliament passed a Highways Act that enabled parishes to set up highways boards, and another Highways Act in 1862 enabled highways districts to be created. A new administrative body which was to become the most common, the local board, was created by the 1848 Public Health Act and the 1858 Local Government Act. Operating mostly outside the municipal boroughs, there were over 700 local boards in existence by the 1870s. Finally, to complete the picture of administrative confusion, the 1870 Education Act set up school boards in both urban and rural areas. It must be remembered that this new pattern of specialist agencies was imposed upon an England in which the traditional county, parochial and even in some cases manorial system still operated.

From the 1870s an attempt was made to rationalize English local government. In 1871, following the report of the 1869 Royal Sanitary Commission, a special ministry, the Local Government Board, was created to oversee local administration in all its facets. The 1872 Public Health Act created urban and rural sanitary authorities in order to cover the whole country with a uniform public health administration. In the 1880s it was clear that some fundamental and organic change would have to be made and, under pressure from Joseph Chamberlain, it appeared likely that Gladstone's ministry would introduce major legislation. However, the priority given to suffrage reform, added to the 1886 Irish crisis, which split the Liberals, meant that in the event it was Salisbury's Conservative government that introduced the 1888 County Councils Act, which finally created an effective local government system for the whole country (Dunbabin, 1963).

Three important points must be made about the origin of the 1888 Act. First, it lay in the logic of 1835. The principles of representative local government could not forever be denied to the county, and Francis Place had anticipated that the municipal idea would eventually become universal. As he told Parkes after the first municipal elections, 'the time shall come, as soon it must, and that too at no great distance, and the *whole* country shall be municipalized . . . I believe we shall have an incorporation of the whole country which will be the basis of a purely representative government.'[2] Radicals, both philosophical and political, would have preferred a national system in 1835. To the Benthamites it was most logical that all areas should be treated the same, and to the political Radicals the extension of democracy into the countryside would be a blow at landed rule. The Radical MP, Joseph Hume, introduced a measure for the establishment of elected county boards both in the 1830s and 1840s. There were no less than seven private bills proposed for elected county government between 1836 and 1869 and in the 1870s two government measures, all of which failed.

The landed gentry were far more resistant to change than Place had anticipated, and they remained as *appointed* county governors for over half a century after 1835. Indeed John Stuart Mill found the county bench of Quarter Sessions the most reactionary aspect of the English constitution:

> The mode of formation of these bodies is most anomalous, they being neither elected, nor in any proper sense of the term, nominated, but holding their important functions, like the feudal lords whom they succeeded, virtually by right of their acres . . . The institution is the most aristocratic in principle which now remains in England; far more so than the House of Lords. . . . It is clung to with proportionate tenacity by our aristocratic classes; but it is obviously at variance with all the principles which are the foundations of representative government.[3]

The more democratic other institutions became the more anomalous the county bench appeared, and when in 1884 the rural labourers obtained the Parliamentary franchise it was inevitable that elected county government must soon follow. It was hardly sensible to say that the farm labourer was qualified to have a view on British foreign policy but not on the parish pump.

If 1888 lay in the logic of democracy, it originated secondly, in the very lack of logic of the local government system which had developed. There was a multiplicity of overlapping areas, competing authorities and fragmented jurisdictions. As Gladstone's minister, G. J. Goschen, asserted in 1871, 'we have a chaos as regards authorities, a chaos as regards rates and a worse chaos than all as regards areas.' A person lived under a mind-boggling mixture of authorities. Standing in one place he could be simultaneously in a parish, borough and county (the historic divisions), a Poor Law union, a local board district and a school board district, and in rural areas might also be in a registration district, a highways district and a sanitary area. It was common for a Poor Law union to contain within it a borough council, two or three local boards, a highways board, a school board, as well as a board of guardians. In the 1870s and 1880s there was so much general awareness of the evils of this confused system, so many Parliamentary and government discussions that reform was by then inevitable.

The growth of democracy and the practical defects made organic change irresistible, but the form of that change was determined by municipal progress over half a century. The principles implanted into county government in 1888 were not simply those of 1835, but those which municipalities had spawned and nurtured from 1835 onwards. Municipal government of 1885 was very different from that of 1835, and it was the 1885 model that was copied, not the frail prototype of 1835. Through time the principles of 1835 had been tried and tested and had been found, in amended and augmented form, to be appropriate to local needs. Already in 1868 one municipal reformer could argue that:

> The trial of the modern system has been conclusive as to its general success and satisfactory operation. Everywhere the dwellers in the large towns have experienced the advantages accruing from the management of public property, the regulation of local police and the adjustments of their various affairs, by responsible representative bodies. . . . The period in which the idea was possible of retaining men in a condition of pupilage is passing away; and it is now felt more or less that men are everywhere entitled to the rights of citizenship.[4]

So in 1888 those rights of citizenship were extended into the county areas. Sixty-three county councils were established by the 1888 Act, and perhaps more important, sixty-one boroughs were exempted from county rule and became county boroughs. The Local Government Act of 1894 completed the municipalization of English local government by the creation of Urban and Rural District Councils to succeed the former urban and rural sanitary authorities. The 1894 Act also revived the parish as a unit of administration by establishing parish councils. Thus, in the words of Redlich and Hirst, 'the broad democratic principles of the Municipal Corporations Act were at last applied and extended in full to the smallest units of government.'

It was the municipal experience of the great cities that had rendered county government by the J.P.s abhorrent, and it was the practical operation of municipal reform that posed so stark a contrast with the regime of the county bench. No group saw this more clearly than the Chamberlainite Radicals within Gladstonian Liberalism. Having seen in Chamberlain's mayoralty in Birmingham the potential of effective local government, they were anxious to press the government to extend these advantages to the counties. Chamberlain included elected county government in his electrifying campaign in 1885 for the 'unauthorized programme', and in the parallel *Radical Programme*, published during the same election, the central point was well made:

> In the large towns no serious fault can be found with the working of the system . . . it has proved an educational agency of the highest value. It has elicited and nurtured qualities in the case of individuals which might otherwise have languished for lack of opportunity; it has opened the way from parochial politics to Imperial statesmanship; its discipline, its competition, its stimulus, have invested those who have actively taken part in it with a dignity of a solid and energising kind. The great corporations, conducted as they are with marked, intelligence, have been instrumental in bestowing the utmost advantage on the population. The field of their responsibilities has been for years steadily on the increase, and at each step their functions and powers have been proportionally enlarged. Much, however, yet remains to be done. . . . it is only a section of the inhabitants of Great Britain itself which enjoys the benefits of local government at all. . . . the most grievous defects of our present system are to be found in the rural districts, where local government properly so-called hardly exists at all . . . where the paramount authority—that of the Quarter Sessions—has no representative character.[5]

By 1885, when those words were written, English urban authorities had become institutions with wide social purposes and they really did conduce to the general welfare of the local community. And the process of becoming so lay at the heart of the municipal revolution, which this book's case studies have sought to illuminate. The answer to the municipal question — in Parkes's phrase, 'what our civic institutions are and what they should be'—surely lies in the experiences of the towns we have studied and the virtue of a comparative treatment is that it allows us to isolate the idiosyncratic from the universal. Having asserted at the outset that the establishment and growth of municipal authority in nineteenth-century England can only be mapped and understood in its local context, we are now, after exploring the municipal history of seven towns, in a position to make some judgments about the municipal revolution in Victorian England. Perhaps we can say no more than that each town had its own unique story to tell and that there were as many variations on the municipal theme as there were towns. If this were so then it would be a valid but disappointing conclusion to draw from a comparative study of English municipal history. However, the thickness of the local foliage cannot completely hide the shape of the municipal tree, and there were components in the municipal revolution which we can identify as pretty well universal. The book's comparative case studies yield a picture of a municipal revolution which comprised three essential facets the establishment of the authority of municipal councils, the creation and accumulation of powers and the definition of a positive social role in municipal affairs.

THE ESTABLISHMENT OF MUNICIPAL AUTHORITY

The establishment of the authority of municipal councils itself involved three developments. The first and fundamental prerequisite was the confirmation of the legal status of town councils, as vital to those boroughs listed in the 1835 Act as to those later incorporated. The Municipal Corporations Act had been approved by crown, lords and commons so that there could be no question mark over the existence of the new councils, but there was doubt over their relationship to the old corporations and their properties. When unreformed corporations disposed of their property in order to prevent it falling into the hands of their successors were they alienating assets which were inviolate? Were the councils entitled to inherit these assets? The Act appeared to be unequivocal and it laid down that corporate properties were to pass down to the elected councils. Yet as we saw, it required legal action in both Leeds and Liverpool for the new councils there to acquire their due inheritance. This was akin to a symbolic test case of the moral and legal authority of municipal councils, and when Leeds Town Council won its case in 1840 it was a vindication of the legal status of municipal councils generally. As is well known, the legal position of newly incorporated towns was far more problematical. For five years the councils of Manchester, Birmingham and Bolton laboured under a very dark legal cloud, deprived even of the right to run their own police forces. Had their charters not been confirmed then the 1835 municipal revolution would indeed have been still-born. As it was, the decision in the test case, *Rutter v Chapman*, not only established the legality of these three charters; it also confirmed the procedure by which other towns might now be incorporated in a legally sound way.

To legal authority had to be added, secondly, social authority through status and prestige. The social position of town councils in urban society could be established only by the participation of the leading citizens in the urban community. Sometimes, as in Leeds or Bradford, the frustrated social ambitions of economic leaders was sufficient to establish the council immediately as the natural location of social leadership in the city. Seats on the council, aldermanic robes, the mayoral chain and even a place on the magisterial bench were sufficiently alluring to induce the wealthy and respectable of a town to seek municipal office. By so doing they enshrined the council with the aura of social authority and made it the political expression of the urban elite. Even when, as sometimes happened, the first flush of municipal enthusiasm was dulled, and the social quality of council membership declined, the social authority of the municipal council could never become completely tarnished, for there was always the precedent of municipal service which could be cited to inspire future generations. It was far more difficult, as in Birmingham or Sheffield, where there was a marked indifference and even hostility towards municipal service by the urban elite. There it required some major breakthrough to designate council membership as a legitimate and respectable aspiration for an urban gentleman. In Birmingham council service was made a religious imperative in the 1860s and 1870s, with startling effects upon the social composition and municipal policy of the council. In Sheffield it was widely acknowledged that the virtual irrelevance of the council was wholly due to the history of its social composition, that, as one observer recorded, 'the main reason for the degradation of the council has been that the intellect and property of the town has stood aloof from it.' It was not just that leading business and professional men gave an aura of respectability to a council. They also brought business acumen, an enlarged municipal vision and organizational talent. The remark in Birmingham in the 1850s that spending large sums of municipal money 'filled the brewer, the baker and the candlestick maker with alarm' was neatly echoed in Salford a decade later when an anonymous citizen confirmed that 'it would be as unreasonable to expect the small trader who deals in units of tens and seldom reaches three figures, to comprehend sums involving some hundreds of thousands, as it would be to expect a man ignorant of geometry and mathematics to calculate the distance and density of Saturn.'[6] A middle-class elite endowed the council with social authority and with the potential of an augmented field of municipal usefulness.

Paradoxically, uniformly elitist municipal authorities would have emulated one of the unreformed corporations' worst defects—remoteness from their local community. To prevent a new form of oligarchy, municipal reform had to forge a strong link between the council and its community, and this was the third element in the establishment of municipal authority. The council had to become a focus of citizenship as well as a fount of social authority. The council had to personify *civitas* for all its citizens. This was to be achieved initially through election, which would make the council the true representative of its municipality. And whatever actually ensued, it was the clear intention of Whig ministers that the municipal franchise should be more democratic than the Parliamentary. As one of them recorded in his diary:

> Decided . . . in favour of resident three year ratepayers instead of ten pounders. I think this is right. It is necessary to confine votes for the management of their own funds to the same class, and it is wholesome that the voters for Parliament should be taught that they have not a monopoly of all rights — that others, incapable of voting on these occasions, yet enjoy privileges, and that it was not the intention of Parliament in extending the franchise to create any species of oligarchy in the country.[7]

It should also be noted that the municipal franchise was more democratic than the multiple voting based on property ownership which both the 1834 Poor Law Amendment Act and the 1848 Public Health Act inherited from Sturges Bourne's Act of 1818. As Cobden frequently remarked, there was no Sturges Bourne 'bricks against brains' in the 1835 Act which he deemed 'the most democratic measure upon our statute book.'

In practice the residence and ratepaying qualifications reduced the actual municipal electorate, often below that of the £10 Parliamentary franchise. However, in some places a good deal of discretion was exercised in drawing up the burgess roll, and so franchise limitations did not prevent Chartists from entering the councils of Leeds and Sheffield in some numbers during the 1840s. More important, the worst effects of the qualification restricting the vote to personal ratepayers (thus disfranchising the so-called compounders whose rates were paid by landlords) were removed by the passing of the Small Tenements Rating Act in 1850. This allowed the rating of cheap properties, often not rated before, and protected tenants by ensuring that occupiers whose rates had been paid would obtain the municipal franchise. It was a permissive act, but where it was adopted it more than doubled the municipal electorate.

This enlarged electorate created the community of interests

between the council and its municipality on the Benthamite principle that what was participated in by all would conduce to the benefit of all. It was the possibilities of general participation which did most to establish the council as the focus of citizenship. The reformer already quoted who in 1867 argued that 'the trial of the modern system has been conclusive,' wished to extend municipalization to the rest of the country and he stressed its role in encouraging citizenship:

> To afford a channel in which the political energies of townsmen may legitimately flow is a thing to be desired; and that channel the incorporation of smaller towns, with the accompanying impartation of citizenship, would provide. By offering to the dwellers in every populous community the opportunity of the exercise of a municipal franchise, the state would furnish in truth a 'safety valve' for the outlet of the increasing political energy of the people of this country. Not alone would a more impartial administration of local affairs be secured—not alone would a desirable employment of public spirit be presented—by the erection of municipalities in every district of this kingdom, the sense of local interest and self respect of the townsmen would also find their legitimate gratification in the ability to elect, and the possibility of being elected, managers of their own local affairs.[8]

As Chamberlain said, and his career demonstrated, municipal councils opened up the way from parochial to imperial politics.

We must not underestimate the role of politics in ensuring popular participation, for in many ways the creation of the council as the focus of citizenship was a reflection of the degree to which the council had become a political forum. We saw how municipal reform itself and later incorporations were perceived as essentially political controversies, and municipal policy was often politically highly sensitive. There is perhaps a tendency to regard the politicizing of municipal councils as a retrograde development which somehow dissipated municipal energies that might otherwise have been diverted into channels socially more useful. Yet the historian of the most notable self-consciously non-political council, Manchester (Simon, 1938, 398), remarked that some found 'in those councils which are run on party lines . . . a greater sense of responsibility both in office and in opposition than can exist in Manchester.' Politics often generated the spark of municipal interest and participation, and it will not be forgotten that Chamberlain's civic renaissance was originated and sustained by a caucus bent on politicizing all local institutions, with clearly defined political purposes. The connection between political commitment and municipal activity has been well illustrated in a recent study of Cardiff (Daunton, 1977, 166–70). There the council was shunned by the local elite for several decades and was a mere backwater in Cardiff's affairs. A remarkable transformation took place in the 1870s which energized the council, and it originated in the long running battle with the largest local landowner, the Earl of Bute, who dominated the town. When the council was made the focus of this crucial political battle between a town and its quasi-feudal overlord, then the council's membership and functions were drastically changed. The mingling of the political and the municipal elevated corporate horizons. As one reformer explained at a municipal election:

> Influential as his lordship is, there are other matters to be considered, and nobler purposes to be subserved, than the development of his property and the extension of his influence. Cardiff is a rising place and the corporation must keep pace with the times. The lighting and general condition of the streets, the sanitary defects of many houses, the want of adequate attention to the appearance of the town, and a lack of public institutions, all indicate a sluggish action on the part of the corporation, and the absence of that healthy public spirit and zealous pride in local affairs on the part of municipal authorities which are of far more value to a borough than a dozen noblemen and an army of obsequious agents.[9]

Politics often gave sparkle and cutting edge to municipal affairs, thereby identifying the council as the central institution of town life. In summary, then, the establishment of the authority of municipal councils involved the confirmation of the legal status of councils, their establishment as the fount of social authority and the acknowledgement of the council as a focus of citizenship.

THE CREATION AND ACCUMULATION OF POWERS

The question now arises as to what these councils, their legal social and political authority confirmed, could actually do and so we must turn to our second major component, the creation and accumulation of powers. It is necessary at this stage to understand the nature of English law in the nineteenth century. Continental jurists would have expected some legal definition of municipal reform in terms of functions which would have determined just what powers municipal councils had. Having defined the purposes, it would then have been for courts to decide whether actions were legitimate in the light of the defined functions and responsibilities. English law did not operate in this way, for nineteenth-century England had no *droit administratif*, the system of delegated legislation by which administrative bodies made regulations that had the force of law (a system that grew rapidly in the twentieth century). A municipal council had only those powers specifically allocated to it by Parliament. Only by the express provision of the statutory law could a council exercise its functions. So the powers implicit in municipal reform were solely those which were contained in the 1835 Act itself.

There was a possibility that the Whig ministry might introduce one comprehensive bill encompassing a code of powers and functions to apply to corporations generally. Roebuck, as a Benthamite, was convinced that this was the most logical and most desirable approach. He was equally convinced that Parliamentary legislators would be unable or unwilling to meet the challenge of drafting such a complex bill. They would, he predicted, list a number of random functions to which was added 'a drag-net to catch any forgotten or stray rights which may have escaped the detail.' This would lead to never-ending litigation, so that nobody would know just what powers were legal. Roebuck, tongue in cheek, explained why this confusion would not be averted:

> To avoid these mischiefs by a previous, complete and exhaustive classification of the rights and obligations necessary to the end in view, will, we fear, never suggest itself to those whose business it

will be to prepare a bill . . . To do so would appear too much like the conduct of a philosopher; and a philosopher, as every blockhead is supposed to know, and always asserts, is not a practical man. The practical men are the drag-net framers. . . . Would that we could reasonably hope that, in the case of Corporation Reform, science was about to assume its proper function and order and logic to occupy the place of a confused and disorderly enumeration.[10]

As Roebuck anticipated, the all-embracing general act did not materialize, and the 1835 Act endowed the new councils with very limited powers. Lord Morpeth later admitted that the Whigs were wary of empowering councils with wide functions for fear of their political character. The 1835 Act did not prescribe a positive role for councils, many of which were somewhat worse off after 1835 than before. Where, for instance, corporations had wide-ranging duties relating to charities, they lost these functions to local charity commissions and so had a reduced field of activity. The lack of a clear legal prescription for corporate activity is the most important single factor to weigh against the Webbs' notion of a municipal revolution in 1835. Without adequate powers the councils were unable to fulfil the promise of municipal reform, and that is why it was asserted that the municipal revolution in Leeds dated not from 1835 but from 1842, when the Council acquired a powerful improvement act.

Lacking powers under the 1835 Act itself, councils had to accumulate them through time by other means. They did so partly through general adoptive and later compulsory legislation. From the 1840s, Parliament passed a number of permissive acts, which councils could adopt if they so wished. The Town Clauses Acts, the first of which was passed in 1845, established a number of model clauses which local authorities might adopt or include in their own private acts. Similarly the Public Health Act of 1848 enabled councils to operate as local boards of health and thereby to acquire certain public health powers. From the 1870s, particularly from the 1875 Public Health Act, councils were given compulsory duties in the sanitary field with the appropriate powers. Important as these general acts were, far more progress was made by exploiting the traditional and well-established system of private bill legislation, where councils sponsored their own acts with specific powers for their own boroughs. This was, in the words of Redlich and Hirst, 'the most vigorous and fruitful factor in the development and extension of municipal government.'

Local acts provided towns with much individual initiative and allowed them to develop their own particular programmes of reform. Usually the local acts were in advance of general legislation, which then belatedly caught up by legalizing universally what was already local practice. We have recently been reminded (Keith-Lucas, 1977, 15) how many novel powers are to be found in the local acts of the early Victorian years. They included the prohibition of new houses without privies and drains, the banning of cellar dwellings, the provision of public lavatories, gardens and recreation grounds, and the licensing and control of lodging houses, brothels and gaming houses. Even in the last quarter of the century, when general government legislation invaded the municipal field, councils preferred to operate under local acts over which they had some control. By the end of the century Parliament was handling some three hundred local acts per year. The preference for local acts can be accounted for in terms of local pride, local knowledge and local incentive. Beyond this lay a dislike of centralization — the effects of which in stimulating local action have never been properly appreciated. Because English history is primarily written from a national standpoint, from Parliament looking outwards, the anti-centralization sentiment so rife in the mid-nineteenth century has been assessed in terms of its effects upon central institutions. Hence we refer to the practical limits upon the Poor Law Commission, or the watering down of the powers of the General Board of Health caused by anti-centralization feeling. That same popular feeling was also the origin of much positive municipal action, for in defending municipal sovereignty and local control, municipal reformers were anxious to demonstrate by precept that municipalities had no need of central direction. They wished to show that their own borough should always be exempt from the provisions of impending legislation, and the best way of so doing was to operate their own local administrative system. The four great definitive local acts, Leeds 1842, Manchester 1844, Liverpool 1846 and Birmingham 1851, all owed something to a desire by the metropolitan cities to be free of central control. The hostility of centralization thus not only delayed and restricted the growth of central administrative bodies, but also accelerated the proliferation of local acts that spread increased powers throughout the municipalities.

Through local acts the town councils of England became all-purpose and all-powerful local authorities, sovereign in their own domain. We might view this as a near-inevitable process, but most contemporaries would not have regarded it so. There were rivals to the municipal council, such as improvement commissions, highways boards and other township institutions. On the sometimes specious argument of administrative specialization (which Parliament encouraged outside the boroughs) these bodies defended their petty sovereignty against municipal encroachment. Similarly, the historical geography of most towns encouraged a sense of township or suburban loyalty which was resistant to what can only be termed local centralization. If councils were to become effective masters in their own house, they would have to undermine parochialism, and so an essential feature of the accumulation of powers was the process of amalgamation, both of powers and of institutions. The 1835 Act had made only the most hesitant of steps in this direction, and, as anti-municipal activists were always quick to point out, very few local bodies took the opportunity to merge with the new councils by the voluntary procedures laid down in the act. Leeds was typical of many cities in that one act in 1842 amalgamated the improvement commission in the council and another in 1866 amalgamated the highways board. Of course, the classic battles over amalgamation were fought out in Birmingham in the 1840s and Sheffield in the 1850s. Birmingham Town Council had to combat a respected improvement body, the Street Commission, and the particularism of the township institutions. Deritend and Bordesley were within a mile of the Birmingham city centre, but they still preferred township to borough sovereignty. In

Sheffield a prolonged battle was fought between municipal government and township anarchy when Isaac Ironside maintained that true democracy began in the vestry institutions. Though Toulmin Smith was Ironside's hero and mentor, he had in the Birmingham dispute firmly backed municipal sovereignty — 'all the power of all Commissioners and local boards must be vested in the Town Council.' The success of amalgamation may be measured by the fact that in 1879 only 14 out of 240 municipal boroughs still had a sanitary authority outside the town council. So by amalgamation, many local acts and a few adoptive general acts, powers were created and accumulated for councils to adopt the role of the 'municipal Leviathan.'

THE DEFINITION OF A POSITIVE SOCIAL ROLE

What councils would do with their powers, indeed the nature of the powers themselves, was totally dependent upon our third factor, the definition of a positive social role in municipal affairs. It has been well said that there was never a theory of collectivism to rival the philosophy of laissez-faire (MacDonagh, 1977, 20-1), for collectivism simply evolved out of the purely pragmatic response of the Victorian state to urban social problems. And so it was with municipal welfare. The municipal revolution progressed by stages as councils took practical steps to face practical problems in their boroughs, and by so doing they committed their corporations ever more deeply to interventionist policies. Again and again we found that municipal reform came to define its purpose in public health. The responsibility for the general welfare of the community, which was the ultimate social purpose that late Victorian councils acknowledged, originated in an early Victorian commitment to environmental control.

There were municipal reformers who had struggled to produce some rational basis for this municipal activity — The 'Philosophic' Radicals, Baker in Leeds, Shimmin in Liverpool, Redfern in Birmingham, Winks in Leicester, and many others. Yet they had done so in the most general terms of the municipal responsibility, for whatever was conducive to the community's best interests. It was on the practical plane rather than the theoretical that municipal reform was measured, and it was noticeable that when Mayor Alexander Kay reviewed the achievements of Manchester Town Council after its seven year apprenticeship he did so in terms of the practical improvements the Council had introduced into town life. He concluded significantly, 'we have acquired the power . . . of promoting the health and comforts of our population.'[11] The first successful attempt to create a philosophy of municipal reform was the Birmingham 'civic gospel.' Perceptive and inspring as that was, we have to note that it was the articulation in moral and religious terms of a concept which was already well rooted in municipal practice, elsewhere if not in Birmingham. It was in the very nature of the environmental problems that the attempt at their solution would draw councils further along the collectivist road. By trial and error, councils found that they always needed to increase their powers because the problems were never as responsive to legislative treatment as was first anticipated, and so there was a never-ending process of amending private legislation, which always augmented municipal powers. As we saw in Liverpool, the people driven out of cellars flocked into the alleys; the control of the alleys flooded the cheap housing market; so in the end the desire for sanitary regulation forced the council to consider the provision of housing. The purchase of a magnificent park in Leeds five miles from the city centre eventually committed the council to providing a public transport system to enable citizens to make use of it.

Perhaps it is correct to regard the initial phase of public health as one stage and the wider provision of parks, libraries, swimming baths and the rest as a second stage: 'sanitation' first and 'civilization' second (Meller, 1976, 237). However, it is probably more valuable to think in terms of a gradually widening definition of the social purposes of muncipal reform. The commitment to environmental control was crucial, and the desire to create a decent wholesome environment simply encompassed broader horizons as time went on. In early Victorian England the wholesome environment was seen mainly in terms of sanitary regulation, while by the later Victorian years it had been perceived as supplying men's cultural and recreational needs as well. As Chamberlain so powerfully argued, sanitary and educational reform were but two sides of the same coin. The broader attack upon the problems of town life began, as the Bristol sanitary reformer Willian Budd said in 1869, with an attack upon the citizens' liberty, 'the sacred liberty to poison not only themselves but their neighbours also.'[12] The antidote to this poison in the form of a dose of Chamberlainism transformed the municipal image. A review of Birmingham municipal affairs in 1878 demonstrated how much councils had changed from their original Whig conception of representative institutions for the maintenance of urban order:

> The government of the town is in its own hands free, unfettered and complete. We have public edifices not unworthy of the place. Our streets are well kept, lighted, drained and watched. We have the means for the administration of justice by our own magistrates and in our own courts. The monopolies of gas and water have ceased to exist: these undertakings have passed into the hands of the community. The health of the population is cared for by an efficient system of sanitary measures; the means of cleanliness are afforded by baths and wash-houses; recreation is provided by parks and pleasure grounds; and the opportunities of culture are offered to all classes in free libraries and museums of art. These benefits result directly from the institution of corporate government, and by such an agency alone could the force and the means of the community be directed to purposes of general advantage.[13]*

From the 1870s these wider social purposes were increasingly evident, and by the 1890s the change through practical commitment was clear to all. Everywhere the wider definition of a municipal social role was enlarging the services the council provided for its citizens. As one observer noticed in 1895,

*The extension of municipal activity can also be seen in the growth of borough debts. Figures for 1885 were Birmingham £7.0m, Manchester £6.9m, Liverpool £5.8m., Leeds £4.0m., Bradford £4.0m., Leicester £1.3m.

> The larger provincial towns are . . . laying out parks and playgrounds using in fact municipal funds to increase the pleasure and health of the community . . . the future of life in large cities may be contemplated with the assurance that it will be brighter, sweeter and more appreciative of the necessities of modern life and more anxious to adopt improvements that will add to the happiness of the communities they represent.[14]

The commitment to happiness would take municipalities towards the next logical step, the idea of town planning, which grew rapidly in the early years of the twentieth century. The council would not so much make possible a wholesale environment through regulation; it would plan and build the wholesome environment itself and it would be so created that the social evils of urbanization would disappear. As the Birmingham pioneer J. S. Nettlefold argued in 1908:

> We cannot by legislation make people healthy and happy but we can give our town dwellers fewer temptations to irrational excitement and more opportunities for beneficial enjoyment than they have at present. We can, if we will, let light and air into our towns; we can, if we will make the most and not the least of the sunshine.[15]

In the ideal city of the future the municipality would replace urban squalor with the garden suburb.

What had no philosophy could hardly be deemed ideological yet paradoxically it became so. In the 1890s and early 1900s what was increasingly being dubbed 'municipal socialism' was a matter of great ideological debate. Indeed just when Redlich and Hirst's book appeared which argued that the battle of municipal reform was over, that the whole of local government had been municipalized, a major propaganda war was in full flow over the ideology of municipal welfare. These ideological overtones were imparted to the municipal question from opposite directions. The growing Labour movement adopted municipal socialism partly to get Labour members elected onto councils and partly as a means of maintaining socialist faith by establishing a programme of achievable practical objectives (such as school meals or educational grants). At the opposite end of the political spectrum, the extreme right tried to rouse public opinion from a slumber during which, they claimed, municipal socialism appeared to be undermining capitalism without anyone's noticing it. The idea of municipal activity conquering *laissez-faire* by stealth was never better captured than in Sidney Webb's famous description of the individualist town councillor who would

> walk along the municipal pavement, lit by municipal gas and cleansed by municipal brooms with municipal water, and seeing by the municipal clock in the municipal market that he is too early to meet his children coming from the municipal school, hard by the county lunatic asylum and municipal hospital, will use the national telegraph system to tell them not to walk through the municipal park, but to come by the municipal tramway to meet him in the municipal reading-room by the municipal art gallery, museum and library where he intends to consult some of the national publications in order to prepare his next speech in the municipal town hall in favour of the nationalisation of canals and the increase of Government control over the railway system. 'Socialism, Sir,' he will say, 'don't waste the time of a practical man by your fantastic absurdities. Self-help, Sir, individual self-help, that's what made our city what it is.'[16]

Of course, the moral of Webb's story was that, perhaps by a process of self-deception, urban society had contained the growth of municipal service within a non-ideological mental framework.

There had certainly been some fundamental political debates over the proper role of a municipal council, for instance over water supply in Leeds and Liverpool or over improvement in Leicester and Birmingham, and they had in a sense been fought out between embryonic collectivists and *laissez-faire* capitalists. Yet in those definitive arguments, many who defended the free market system in other matters were in favour of extending municipal control over all sorts of civic affairs, and they certainly did not believe that they were advancing any broad ideological cause. The most celebrated Victorian municipal reformer, Joseph Chamberlain, himself one of Birmingham's wealthiest businessmen, was no socialist, for all his talk of a ransom on the land. It was possible, as we saw, to denote Liverpool's municipal role as 'cradle to grave welfare' without any implication that the Liverpool Town Council was being used as a Fabian Trojan horse. The pragmatic rather than the ideological continued to spur municipal endeavour in both welfare and trading sectors. A growing understanding and awareness of the complexity of urban problems pushed councils towards the wider social functions we noticed in the cultural, recreational, housing and welfare provision of late Victorian and Edwardian municipalities. At the same time municipal trading was an enterprise that advanced almost under its own momentum as technology changed the priorities. When lighting was supplied by gas, councils took gas supply into municipal ownership, partly to serve consumers' interests and partly to subsidize the rates out of gas profits. If it had been right to do that, it followed that it was right to supply electricity when that became a practical possibility. If the citizens were to be protected from a commercial monopoly of gas and water, they ought also to be protected from a commercial monopoly of transport, and so municipal tramways multiplied. If municipalities could provide the public with wash-houses it was equally permissible to provide cold stores, and all these municipal enterprises would have to be run as commercial successes — in effect, public business in competition with private enterprise.

Though there were probably only a few councils such as Bradford where there was a concerted attempt to utilize municipal activity as a socialist weapon, nevertheless the scale of municipal involvement worried many on the right who saw municipal socialism as an insidious form of disruption. So at the end of the century the so-called Liberty and Property Defence League produced a weekly digest of objectionable private bills to be heard in Parliament, and its M.P.s did their best to strike out what were deemed dangerous clauses (Soldon, 1974). It was as much the extent as the nature of municipal enterprise that caused concern, for by 1902, when *The Times* was filled with anti-municipal articles and letters, there were some two hundred municipal gas and water undertakings and over a hundred transport undertakings. It is likely that most citizens turning on a municipal gas or water tap, or catching a municipal tram, or swimming in a municipal bath or borrowing a book from a municipal library, did not consider they were doing anything that had any ideological implication at all. For most people 'gas and water socialism' had little, if anything, to do with socialism. At the same time the controversy over municipal socialism was an indication of how much councils had changed in the fifty or sixty years since 1835. Though of short-term origin, the propaganda war fought out over the heads of active municipalities was a comment on the long-term municipal revolution this book has sought to explain. That revolution had been built on a triple foundation — the establishment of the legal, social and political authority of town councils, the creation and accumulation of municipal powers and the definition of a positive social role for municipal reform. These three carried English municipal authority from the era of corporation reform to the age of municipal socialism.

Notes

CHAPTER ONE

1. *First Report of the Municipal Corporations Commission, Parliamentary Papers* (1835), XXIII, p. 17.
2. J. Parkes to F. Place, 4 Nov. 1833, B.M. Add. Mss. 35149, f. 234; Wellington to J. W. Cooper, B.M. Add. Mss. 38078, ff. 65–7.
3. *First Report*, op. cit., p. 49.
4. J. Parkes to Durham, 1 June 1835, quoted by J. K. Buckley, *Joseph Parkes of Birmingham* (1926), p. 122.
5. J. Parkes to E. J. Stanley, 6 Sept. 1835, Parkes Papers (University College, London).
6. *Hansard's Parliamentary Debates*, 3rd Series, XXIX, 1383, 1401.
7. Sir R. Peel to J. W. Croker, 2 July 1835, L. J. Jennings (ed.), *The Croker Papers* (1884), II, p. 280.
8. Leeds Corporation Court Book 1773–1835, pp. 424–9.
9. J. Parkes to F. Place, 2 Jan. 1836, B.M. Add. Mss. 35150, ff. 99–101.
10. *Birmingham Journal*, 4 Nov. 1837.
11. A Radical Reformer, *Incorporate Your Borough* (Manchester, 1837), pp. 2–6.
12. S. and B. Webb, *Manor and Borough* (1908) II, p. 755; R. A. H. Smith, 'The Passing of the Municipal Corporations Act 1830–1835 . . .' (East Anglia, M.Phil thesis, 1974), p. 86; J. Redlich and F. W. Hirst, *Local Government in England* (1903) I, p. 96.
13. J. A. Roebuck, *The Municipal Elections* in J. A. Roebuck (ed.), *Pamphlets for the People* (1835–6).
14. J. A. Roebuck, *A letter to the Electors of Bath* (15 June 1835), *loc. cit.*
15. *Prospectus of the Municipal Corporation Reformer*, Place Papers, B.M. Add. Mss. 35150, ff. 55–7; cf. F. Place, *The Peers and the People* in Roebuck (ed.) *Pamphlets* . . .

CHAPTER TWO

1. *First Report of Municipal Corporations Commission*, IV (1835), 2706.
2. *Liverpool Mercury*, 25 Oct. 1833.
3. Ibid., 20 Nov. 1835.
4. *First Report of the Royal Commission on the Health of Large Towns and Populous Districts* (1844), Appendix, p. 188.
5. 9 and 10 Victoria, Cap 127, Clause 1.

6. J. Grantham, *On the Supply of Water to Liverpool* (Liverpool, 1848), p. 17; H. Banner, *Water, A Pamphlet* (Liverpool, 1845), p. 18.
7. *R. C. Health of Large Towns* . . . (1844), Appendix p. 193.
8. S. Holme, *Want of Water* (Liverpool, 1845), pp. 53-4.
9. *Liverpool Mail*, 9 May 1846.
10. *Liverpool Mercury*, 25 Sept. 1849.
11. Ibid., 16 Feb. 1849.
12. R. Stephenson, *The Supply of Water to the Town of Liverpool* (1850), pp. 47-8.
13. Health Committee Minutes, 13 Sept. 1849.
14. J. Newlands, *Liverpool Past and Present* . . . (Liverpool, 1859), p. 20.
15. *Porcupine*, 10 Oct. 1863.
16. Ibid., 17 Oct. 1863.
17. H. Shimmin, *The Courts and Alleys of Liverpool* (Liverpool, 1864), p. 67.
18. *Porcupine*, 13 Aug. 1864.
19. *Liverpool Courier*, 5 Aug. 1870.
20. E. F. Rathbone, *William Rathbone, A Memoir* (1908), p. 243.
21. J. Rayner, *Sanitary and Social Improvement* (Liverpool, 1875), p. 8.
22. R. Muir, *A History of Liverpool* (1907), reprinted (Wakefield, 1970), p. 337.

CHAPTER THREE

1. *First Report of the Municipal Corporations Commission*, IV (1835), *Leeds Report*, p. 9.
2. *Leeds Mercury*, 28 Dec. 1833; S. and B. Webb, *Statutory Authorities for Special Purposes* (Reprint 1963), p. 384.
3. J. R. Drinkwater and R. J. Saunders, Report 26 Jan. 1833, P.R.O. HO52/23; *Leeds Report*, p. 6.
4. Leeds Corporation Court Book, 12 June 1835.
5. C. Scarborough, Election handbill 1837 in 'Representation of Leeds 1831-1841' (Thoresby Society Library).
6. *Leeds Intelligencer*, 11 Feb. 1837.
7. *Leeds Mercury*, 16 Jan. 1836.
8. *Leeds Intelligencer*, 5 March 1836.
9. *Leeds Mercury*, 27 Feb. 1836.
10. *Leeds Intelligencer*, 27 Oct. 1838.
11. *Leeds Mercury*, 27 May 1837.
12. Ibid., 2 Nov. 1839.
13. *Leeds Times*, 31 Dec. 1842.
14. *Leeds Intelligencer*, 15 Sept. 1849.
15. Ibid., 6 Sept. 1851.
16. J. Hole, *The Homes of the Working Classes* (1866), p. 94.
17. *Leeds Mercury*, 3 Feb. 1865.
18. Ibid.

19. Hole, *loc. cit.*
20. *Leeds Mercury*, 9 April 1868.
21. Ibid., 9 April 1867.
22. J. S. Curtis, *The Story of the Marsden Mayoralty* (Leeds, 1875), p. 61.

CHAPTER FOUR

1. *Holden's Triennial Directory* (Birmingham, 1805), p. 9; C. Pye, *A Description of Modern Birmingham* (Birmingham, 1818), p. 76.
2. J. A. Langford, *A Century of Birmingham Life* (Birmingham, 1867), II, p. 311.
3. *Birmingham Journal*, 23 Jan. 1836.
4. Ibid., 21 March 1829.
5. Ibid., 15 March 1828.
6. *Aris's Birmingham Gazette*, 3 March 1828.
7. *Birmingham Journal*, 21 Oct. 1837.
8. J. T. Bunce, *History of the Corporation of Birmingham*, I (1878), p. 247.
9. *Birmingham Journal*, 8 July 1831.
10. Ibid., 4 Nov. 1837.
11. *Aris's Birmingham Gazette*, 6 Nov., 25 Dec. 1837.
12. *Ten Objections to the Birmingham Corporation* (Birmingham, 1839), p. 4.
13. *Birmingham Journal*, 10 Nov. 1838; *Birmingham Advertiser*, 28 Dec. 1837.
14. Quoted by C. Gill, *History of Birmingham* (Oxford, 1952), I, p. 228.
15. *Birmingham Journal*, 21 Oct. 1837; *Ten Objections* . . . p. 8.
16. *Birmingham Advertiser*, 27 March 1845; *Aris's Birmingham Gazette*, 13 March 1848.
17. *Birmingham Journal*, 19 July 1845.
18. R. Rawlinson, *Report to the General Board of Health on the Borough of Birmingham* (1849), p. 80.
19. *Birmingham Journal*, 21 July 1849.
20. J. T. Smith, *The Public Health Board and the Surrender of Birmingham* (Birmingham, 1849).
21. J. Postgate, *The Sanatary Aspect of Birmingham and Suggestions for its Improvement* (Birmingham, 1852), p. 14.
22. T. Avery, 'Municipal Expenditure of Birmingham' in British Association, *Report of the Proceedings at the Birmingham Meeting* (1865), p. 298.
23. Quoted by A. Briggs, *Victorian Cities* (1963), p. 208.
24. *Short History of the Passing of the . . . Gas Act and . . . Water Act . . .* (Birmingham, 1875), p. 9.
25. Quoted by A. Briggs, *Victorian Cities* (1963), p. 229 and E. P. Hennock, *Fit and Proper Persons* (1973), p. 126.
26. J. T. Bunce *History of the Corporation of Birmingham*, II (1885), p. XXIV.
27. C. W. Boyd (ed.), *Speeches of Joseph Chamberlain* (1914), I, p. 41.

CHAPTER FIVE

1. G. Bush, *Bristol and Its Municipal Government 1820–1851* (Bristol, 1976), p. 86.
2. *Bristol Times*, 2 Sept. 1854, quoted by D. Large and F. Round, *Public Health in Mid-Victorian Bristol* (Bristol, 1974), p. 11.
3. H. E. Meller, *Leisure and the Changing City, 1870–1914* (1976), p. 115.
4. *First Report of the Municipal Corporations Commission*, XXIII (1835), p. 1909.
5. R. Read, *Modern Leicester* (Leicester, 1881), p. 228; *Leicester Herald*, 22 April 1831.
6. *Leicester Journal*, 26 Oct. 1838.
7. *Leicester Conservative Standard*, Feb. 1836.
8. *Leicester Chronicle*, 21 Sept. 1844.
9. Ibid., 17 Oct. 1846.
10. Ibid., 13 Dec. 1845.
11. Ibid., 27 Dec. 1845.
12. *Report of the National Association for the Promotion of Social Science* (1862), p. 594.
13. *Leicester Chronicle*, 4 Sept. 1852.
14. *Bradford Observer*, 7 Dec. 1843.
15. *Leeds Intelligencer*, 16 Aug. 1845.
16. *Bradford Observer*, 8 April 1847.
17. R. Rawlinson, 'Report on Street Improvements in Bradford,' 3 Feb. 1851, P.R.O. MH13/27, quoted by A. Elliott, 'The Establishment of Municipal Government in Bradford 1837–57' (Bradford Ph.D. thesis, 1976), p. 243.
18. *Bradford Observer*, 11 Nov. 1853.
19. Ibid., 19 Aug. 1852.
20. J. Haywood and W. Lee, *Report of the Sanatory Condition of the Borough of Sheffield* (Sheffield, 1848).
21. *Sheffield and Rotherham Independent*, 9 April 1853.
22. J. Toulmin Smith, *Local Self-Government and Centralisation* (1851), p. 36.
23. Quoted by M. Walton, *Sheffield Its Story and Its Achievements* (Sheffield, 1948), p. 186.
24. *Sheffield Free Press*, 25 Sept. 1852.
25. *Sheffield and Rotherham Indpendent*, 16 Oct. 1858.
26. Ibid., 21 Aug. 1858.
27. Ibid., 8 June 1858.
28. J. M. Furness, *Record of Municipal Affairs in Sheffield* (Sheffield, 1893), p. 113.
29. *Sheffield and Rotherham Independent*, 7 May 1864.
30. Ibid., 7 July 1864.
31. A. J. Mundella to R. E. Leader, 15 Oct. 1871, quoted by D. E. Fletcher, 'Aspects of Liberalism in Sheffield 1849–1886' (Sheffield Ph.D. thesis, 1972), p. 91.

CHAPTER SIX

1. *Leeds Mercury*, 30 April 1836.
2. F. Place to J. Parkes, 3 Jan. 1836, B.M. Add. Mss., 35150, f. 102.
3. J. S. Mill, *Considerations of Representative Government* (1861), Everyman Ed., p. 349.
4. J. Thompson, *An Essay in English Municipal History* (1867), 1971 ed. pp. 193-5.
5. J. Chamberlain et. al., *The Radical Programme* (1885), pp. 235-6.
6. *Salford Weekly News*, 16 July 1864, quoted by J. Garrard, *Leaders and Politics in Nineteenth Century Salford* (Salford, 1977), p. 38.
7. A. D. Kriegel (ed.), *The Holland House Diaries 1831-1840* (1977), p. 303.
8. Thompson, *op. cit.*, p. 196.
9. Quoted by M. J. Daunton, *Coal Metropolis Cardiff 1870-1914* (Leicester, 1977), p. 168.
10. J. A. Roebuck, *A Letter to the Electors of Bath*, 15 June 1835, in J. A. Roebuck (ed.) *Pamphlets for the People* (1835-6).
11. *Manchester Guardian*, 10 Jan. 1846.
12. Speech of W. Budd, *Transactions of the National Association for the Promotion of Social Science* (1869), pp. 386-402.
13. J. T. Bunce, *The History of the Corporation of Birmingham*, I (1878), p. 355.
14. *Western Daily Press*, 11 March 1895, quoted by H. E. Meller, *Leisure and the Changing City 1870-1914* (1976), p. 9.
15. J. S. Nettlefold, *Practical Housing* (1908), p. 46.
16. S. Webb, *Socialism in England* (1889).

Bibliography

CHAPTER ONE

(a) Works cited in the text (bracketed notes)
Finlayson, G. B. A. M. 'The Municipal Corporation Commission and Report, 1833-35', *Bulletin of the Institute of Historical Research*, 36 (1963), pp. 36-52.
— 'The Politics of Municipal Reform, 1835', *English Historical Review*, LXXXI (1966), pp. 673-92.
Gash, N. *Politics in the Age of Peel* (1953).
Keith-Lucas, B. *The English Local Government Franchise, A Short History* (Oxford, 1952).
Peardon, T. 'Bentham's Ideal Republic,' *Canadian Journal of Economics and Political Science*, XVII (1951), pp. 184-203.
Roberts, D. 'Jeremy Bentham and the Victorian Administrative State,' *Victorian Studies*, II (1959), pp. 192-210.
Webb, S., and B. Webb. *English Local Government, The Manor and the Borough* (1908).

(b) Other works
Gross, C. *A Bibliography of British Municipal History* (2nd ed. Leicester, 1966).
Laski, H. J., W. I. Jennings and W. A. Robson (eds.). *A Century of Municipal Progress* (1935).
Martin, G. H., and S. McIntyre. *A Bibliography of British and Irish Municipal History (Leicester, 1972).*
Merewether, H. A., and A. J. Stephens. *The History of the Boroughs and Municipal Corporations of the United Kingdom* (1835).
Redlich, J., and F. W. Hirst. *Local Government in England* (1903).
Smellie, K. B. *A History of Local Government* (1968).
Spencer, F. H. *Municipal Origins* (1911).

CHAPTER TWO

(a) Works cited in text (bracketed notes)
Baines, T. *History of the Commerce and Town of Liverpool* (1852).
Chadwick, E. *Report on the Sanitary condition of the Labouring Population of Great Britain* (1842), Reprinted Edinburgh 1965.
Cockcroft, W. R. 'The Liverpool Police Force 1836-1902,' in S. P. Bell (ed.), *Victorian Lancashire* (Newton Abbot, 1974), pp. 150-68.

Frazer, W. M. *Duncan of Liverpool* (1947).
Lovell, J. *Municipal Government in Liverpool* (Liverpool, 1885).
McGowen, W. T. *Sanitary Legislation with Illustrations from Experience in Liverpool* (Liverpool, 1859).
Muir, R. *A History of Liverpool* (1907), reprinted Wakefield 1970.
Murphy, J. *The Crucial Experiment* (Liverpool, 1959).
Newlands, J. *Liverpool Past and Present in Relation to Sanitary Operations* (Liverpool, 1859).
Parkes, E.A., and J. B. Sanderson. *Report on the Sanitary Condition of Liverpool* (Liverpool, 1871).
Picton, J. A. *Liverpool Improvements and How to Accomplish Them* (Liverpool, 1853).
Rathbone, E. A. *William Rathbone A Memoir* (1908).
Shimmin, H. *The Sanitary Aspect of Philanthropy* (Liverpool, 1866).
Vigier, F. *Change and Apathy* (Massachusetts, 1970).
White, B. D. *A History of the Corporation of Liverpool* (Liverpool, 1951).

(b) Other works
Finch, J. *Statistics of Vauxhall Ward* (Liverpool, 1842).
Fraser, D. *Urban Politics in Victorian England* (Leicester, 1976).
Hume, A. *Condition of Liverpool* (Liverpool, 1858).
Hyde, E. *Liverpool and the Mersey* (Newton Abbot, 1971).
McCabe, A. T. 'The Standard of Living on Merseyside 1850-1875' in S. P. Bell, *Victorian Lancashire* (Newton Abbot, 1974), pp. 127-49.
Midwinter, E. *Old Liverpool* (Newton Abbot, 1971).
Picton, J. A. *Memorials of Liverpool* (1875).
Walmsley, H. M. *Life of Joshua Walmsley* (1879).

CHAPTER THREE

(a) Works cited in the text (bracketed notes)
Baker, R. 'Report upon the condition of the Town of Leeds . . .,' *Journal of the Statistical Society*, II (1839), pp. 5-40.
Barber, B. J. 'Leeds Corporation 1835-1905' (Unpublished Ph.D thesis, University of Leeds 1975).
Braithwaite, J. *An Inquiry into the Causes of the High Death Rate in Leeds* (Leeds, 1865).
Briggs, A. *Victorian Cities* (1963).
Harrison, J. F. C. *James Hole and Social Reform in Leeds* (Leeds, 1954).
Hennock, E. P. *Fit and Proper Persons* (1973).
R. J. Lambert, *Sir John Simon* (1963).
Redlich, J. and F. W. Hirst. *Local Government in England* (1903).
Storch, R. D. 'The Plague of Blue Locusts, Police Reform and Popular Resistance in Northern England 1840-1857,' *International Review of Social History*, XX (1975), pp. 61-90.
Thoresby Society Publications, LIII (1970), pp. 50-81.

Wardell, J. *Municipal History of the Borough of Leeds* (1846).
Wilson, R. G. *Gentlemen Merchants* (Manchester, 1971).

(b) Other works
Beresford, M. W., and G. R. J. Jones, *Leeds and its Region* (Leeds, 1967).
Fraser, D. *Urban Politics in Victorian England* (Leicester, 1976).
Hunter, H. J. 'On the Sanitary State of Leeds' in *Eighth Report of the Medical Officer of the Privy Council* (1866).
Mayhall, J. *Annals of Yorkshire* (1875).
Radcliffe, J. N. *The Sanitary State of Leeds* . . . (1871).
Toft, J. 'Public Health in Leeds in the 19th Century,' (Unpublished M.A. thesis, University of Manchester 1966).
Yorke, H. *A Mayor of the Masses* (Leeds, 1904).

CHAPTER FOUR

(a) Works cited in text (bracketed notes)
Avery, T. *The Corporation of Birmingham and the Water Supply of the Town* (Birmingham, 1869).
Briggs, A. 'Thomas Attwood and the Economic Background to the Birmingham Political Union,' *Cambridge Historical Journal*, IX (1948), pp. 190–216.
— *History of Birmingham* (Oxford, 1952), II.
— *Victorian Cities* (1963).
Bunce, J. T. *History of the Corporation of Birmingham* I (1878), II (1885).
Gill, C. *History of Birmingham* (Oxford, 1952), I.
Hennock, E. P. *Fit and Proper Persons* (1973).
Hutton, W. *History of Birmingham* (Birmingham, 1795).
Stephens, W. B., ed., *Victorian County History, Warwickshire*, VII, *The City of Birmingham* (1964).

(b) Other works
Dale, A. W. W. *The Life of R. W. Dale* (1899).
Garvin, J. L. *The Life of Joseph Chamberlain*, I (1932).
Langford, J. A. *Modern Birmingham and its Institutions* (Birmingham, 1873).
Muirhead, J., (ed.) *Birmingham Institutions* (Birminghan, 1911).
Tholfsen, T. R. 'The Origins of the Birmingham Caucus,' *Historical Journal*, II (1959), pp. 161–84.
Wilson, W. *The Life of George Dawson* (Birmingham, 1905).

CHAPTER FIVE

Bristol
Bush, G. *Bristol and its Municipal Government 1820–1851* (Bristol, 1974).

Large, D., and F. Round *Public Health in Mid-Victorian Bristol* (Bristol, 1974).
Meller, H. E. *Leisure and the Changing City 1870–1914* (1976).
Thomas, S. *The Bristol Riots* (Bristol, 1974).

Leicester
Elliott, M. 'The Leicester Board of Health 1849 to 1872' (Nottingham M.Phil. thesis, 1971).
Greaves, R. W. *The Corporation of Leicester* (1939).
— 'Roman Catholic Relief and the Leicester Election of 1826,' *Trans. Royal Hist. Soc.*, 4th Series, 22 (1940).
Patterson, A. T. *Radical Leicester* (Leicester, 1954).
Plumb, J., ed., *Victoria County History, Leicester*, IV (1958).
Simmons, J. *Leicester Past and Present*, II *Modern City* (1974).
Storey, J. *Historical Sketch of the Borough of Leicester* (Leicester, 1895).

Bradford
Cudworth, W. *Historical Notes on the Bradford Corporation* (Bradford, 1881).
— *Worstedopolis* (Bradford, 1888).
Elliott, A. 'The Establishment of Municipal Government in Bradford 1837–57,' (Bradford Ph.D. thesis, 1976).

Sheffield
Furness, J. M. *Record of Municipal Affairs in Sheffield* (Sheffield, 1893).
Pollard, S. *A History of Labour in Sheffield* (1959).
Salt, J. 'Isaac Ironside 1808–70: The Motivation of a Radical Educationist,' *British Journal of Educational Studies*, XIX (1971).
— 'Experiments in Anarchism 1850–54,' *Trans. Hunter Archaeol. Soc.*, 1972.
Walton, M. *Sheffield Its Story and Its Achievements* (Sheffield, 1948).

CHAPTER SIX

(a) Bracketed notes
Daunton, M. J. *Coal Metropolis Cardiff 1870–1914* (Leicester, 1977).
Dunbabin, J. P. D. 'The Politics of the Establishment of County Councils,' *Historical Journal*, VI (1963), pp. 226–52.
Keith-Lucas, B. *English Local Government in the Nineteenth and Twentieth Centuries* (1977).
Lipman, V. D. *Local Government Areas 1834–1945* (Oxford, 1959).
MacDonagh, O. *Early Victorian Government* (1977).
Meller, H. E. *Leisure and the Changing City* (1976).
Simon S. D. *A Century of City Government* (1938).
Soldon, N. '*Laissez-Faire* as Dogma: The Liberty and Property Defence League, 1882–1914,' in K. D. Brown (ed.) *Essays in Anti-Labour History* (1974).

Somers Vine, J. R. *English Municipal Institutions* (1879).

(b) Other works

Dunbabin, J. P. D. 'Expectations of the New County Councils and their Realization,' *Historical Journal*, VIII (1965), pp. 353-79.

—'British Local Government Reform: The Nineteenth Century and After,' *English Historical Review*, XCII (1977), pp. 777-805.

Fraser, D. *Urban Politics in Victorian England* (Leicester 1976).

Hennock, E. P. *Fit and Proper Persons* (1973).

Keith-Lucas, B. *The English Local Government Franchise* (Oxford, 1951).

Probyn, J. W. (ed.) *Local Government and Taxation in the United Kingdom* (1875).

Redlich, J., and F. W. Hirst. *Local Government in England* (1903).

Young, K. *Local Politics and the Rise of Party* (Leicester, 1975).

Index

Allday, Joseph, 96-9
Althorp, Lord, 5
Argus, The, 96
Attwood, Thomas, 12, 16-17, 20, 80, 84-9 *passim*; Chartism and, 84
Auty, Squire, 132
Avery, Thomas, 96, 99-101, 104-7

Baines, Frederick, 71
Baker, Dr. Robert, 60, 63-4, 167; report on Leeds, 60-1
Barnett, Canon, 119
Bentham, Jeremy, 6, 18
Benthamites, the, 7, 18, 153-4, 161, 163
Biggs, John, 125
Biggs, William, 125-8
Birmingham, 2, 63, 78-110, 114, 123, 131, 142, 150, 158, 166; amalgamation campaign in, 90-5, 96, 108, 166-7; 'Artisans' Dwellings' Act (1875), 108; Bull Ring riots, 89; Chartists in, 84, 88, 89; 'Civic Gospel' of, 101-10, 118, 168; class structure of, 78, 80, 84, 92, 96, 101-3, 159; Court Leet, 79, 83; education in, 90, 104; health and sanitation, 80, 90-110, 169, 171; housing, 93, 108-10; Im-

Birmingham — *continued*
provement Acts, 81, 95, 99: (1828), 81, 82; (1831), 81; (1851), 95, 97; (1875), 108; incorporation of, 83-8, 90; law enforcement in, 88, 89; manorial system in, 79-80; migrants to, 78; municipal franchise, 80, 92, 103-4; Political Union, 7, 12, 16-17, 80, 84-8; prison services, 90; street commission, 81-3, 86, 90-110 *passim*, 117, 166; Town Hall, 82, 83; Waterworks Co., 97
Birmingham Gazette, The, 80
Birmingham Journal, The, 80, 87-8, 91
Birmingham Mercury, The, 94
Birmingham Political Union, 7, 12, 16-17, 80, 84-8
Blackburne, John, 7, 8
'Boar Lane' scheme, The, 72
Bolton, 86, 90, 150, 158
Bradford, 83, 84, 111-48, 150, 158, 169; Chartists in, 132; health and sanitation, 111, 132, 143-39, 172; highways board, 131, 135; housing, 132-3, 136; Improvement Act (1850), 135, 136-7; Improvement commission, 130, 131, 133-4; incor-

Index

Bradford—*continued*
poration of, 111, 131-2, 134; law enforcement, 132; manorial system in, 130; riots in, 132; *Waterworks Act* (1854), 138; Waterworks Co., 137
Brinsley, William, 105
Bristol, 111-48, 149; *Baths and Washhouses Act* (1846), 119; the docks in, 112, 114, 116; health and sanitation, 111, 116-20, 135, 169; *Improvement Act* (1840), 115; incorporation of, 112; law enforcement in, 113, 115; paving commission, 117; political control of, 113-14, 118; public amenities, 119-20; riots in, 113, 115
Bristol riots, 113, 115
Brook, William, 65
Brougham, Lord, 7
Budd, William, 118, 169
Bull Ring riots, 89
Bunce, J. T., 109
Burbidge, Thomas, 123, 124

Cardiff, 162
'*Caucus*', The, 103-4
Cave, Otway, 122
Chadwick, Edwin, 18, 27, 30, 39, 94, 125, 141
Chamberlain, Joseph, 101, 104-10, 156, 161-2, 169, 171-2
Chartered towns, list of, 150
Chartism, 62, 64-5, 69, 84, 88, 89, 132, 140, 160
Cobden, Richard, 17, 20, 132, 139, 160
Cook, William, 105
Cooper, J. A., 134

Coschen, G. J., 154
County Councils Act: (1888), 149, 151-7; (1894), 151-7
County Police Act (1839), 12
Crosskey, H. W., 104

Dale, R. W., 102-3
Davies, Dr. David, 118
Dawson, George, 102-3
Docks, the, 22, 26, 34, 44-5, 112, 114, 116
Douglas, R. K., 87-8, 91
Drinkwater, J. R., 9
Duncan, Dr. William Henry, 27, 30, 36-7, 43
Dunn, Alderman Thomas, 142, 145

Earl of Bute, 162
Eddison, Edwin, 66
Edmonds, George, 85, 88
Education, 19, 25-7, 90, 104
Education Act (1870), 153

Fairbairn, Peter, 67
Farrar, Joseph, 138
Forbes, Henry, 132
Forwood, Sir Arthur, 49
Franchise, the municipal, 9-21 *passim*, 154, 160; Birmingham, 80, 92, 103-4; Leeds, 58, 69-70; Leicester, 126; Liverpool, 23, 25; Sheffield, 142
Free Port Association, the, 116
Fry family, the, 118-19

Gladstone, W. E., 153, 156
Goodman, George, 60
Gordon, Joseph, 130
Graham, Sir James, 6, 90
Grey, Earl, 5, 12, 14

Index

Harris, William, 103
Hawkes, Henry, 99
Health and sanitation, 1, 18, 19, 20, 165, 167–73; *Bath and Washhouse Act* (1846), 119; 'Health of the town' commission: (1842), 27, 28, 45, 125; (1845), 116; *Nuisance Removal Act* (1846), 128; *Public Health Act*: (1848), 1–2, 92, 111, 116–17, 128, 135, 136, 141, 152–3, 160, 164; (1852), 2; (1872), 153; (1875), 164; Royal Sanitary Commission (1869), 153; *Sturges Bourne's Act* (1818), 160; *see also under* Birmingham, Bradford, Bristol, Leeds, Leicester, Liverpool, Sheffield
Highways Act: (1835), 152; (1862), 152
Hirst, F. W., 156, 165, 170
Hobson, Joshua, 64
Hole, James, 71, 128
Holme, Samuel, 27–9, 31–4 *passim*, 45
Hope Shaw, Alderman John, 66–7
Housing, general reform of, 155; *see also under*: Birmingham, Bradford, Leeds, Leicester, Liverpool, Sheffield
Hume, Joseph, 154
Hunter, Dr., 68

Immigration, 30, 36, 39
Incorporation, 1, 2, 11, 17, 111, 157–8; Birmingham, 83–8, 90; Bolton, 86, 90; Bradford, 83, 84, 111, 131–2, 134; Bristol, 112; Leeds, 51, 158; Manchester, 83, 84, 86, 90, Incorporation — *continued* 139; Salford, 83, 84; Sheffield, 111, 139
Ironside, Isaac, 140–7, 167

Jaffray, J. A., 91, 92
Judicial administration, 25, 50, 53–5, 63, 113

Kay, Alexander, 168

Langford, J. A., 79
Leader, Robert, 145
Leeds, 2, 15, 24, 51–77, 81, 95, 112, 114, 166, 168, 169; 'Boar Lane' scheme, 72; borough funds in, 55–8, 73–4; Chartists in, 59, 62, 64–5, 69, 160; class structure of, 51–5, 59, 60–1, 65, 69; health and sanitation, 58–61, 63–8, 69–77, 116, 135, 171; housing, 60, 63, 69, 71, 76; *Improvement Act*: (1842), 62–5, 70; (1866), 71–2; (1869), 72; *Improvement and Gas Act* (1870), 75, 76; Improvement commission (1841), 61–5; incorporation of, 51, 158; judicial administration in, 53–5; law enforcement of, 54, 58–9; municipal franchise in, 62, 69–70; Municipal Reform Association, 73; political composition of council, 57–8, 69, 76–7; prison reform, 58–9, 67; Social Improvement Society, 76; Town hall project, 67; 'Washburn' scheme, 73; *Waterworks Act*: (1837), 65–7; (1867), 72–3
Leeds Mercury, The, 52, 60, 71, 76

188 Index

Leeds Municipal Reform Association, 73
Leicester, 111–48, 169; health and sanitation, 111, 125–30, 135, 143, 171; housing, 129; municipal franchise, 126; political control of, 120–4; public amenities in, 124, 127; Town hall, 126
Leicester Chronicle, The, 125
Liberty and Property Defence League, 172
Linsley, G. A., 73
Liverpool, 2, 22–50, 63, 67, 81, 95, 100, 102, 112, 114, 149, 157, 166, 169; *Building Act* (1842), 39; corporate monopoly in, 22–3; dock administration in, 22, 26, 34, 44–5; educational reform in, 19, 25–7; health and sanitation, 27–44, 48–50, 116, 135, 171; Highways board, 28–9, 30, 32–3; hospital provision, 47–8; housing, 27, 29–30, 39, 40–3, 47–50, 168; law enforcement, 24–5, 29; 'Rivington Pike' scheme, 33–8, 46; *Sanitation Act* (1846), 29–33, 36, 39, 45; *Sanitation Amendment Act* (1864), 39, 42; unemployment in, 40; *Waterworks Act* (1847), 33, 35
Liverpool, Lord, 3
Liverpool Burgess and Ratepayer's Magazine, the, 38
Liverpool Mercury, The, 34–5, 46
Liverpool Satirist, the, 24
Liverpool Tradesmen's Conservative Association, 27–8
Local Government Acts: (1858), 2, 152–3; (1888), 155; (1894), 155–6

Local government board, 153
Lovell, John, 46–7
Lyndhurst, Lord, 7, 10, 13, 15

M'Neile, Rev. Hugh, 25–6
Manchester, 2, 17, 55, 63, 88, 123, 132, 150, 158, 161–2, 166, 168, 169; incorporation of, 83, 84, 86, 87, 139
Melbourne, Lord, 9
Midland Counties Herald, the, 91
Milligan, Robert, 132, 134
Morbidity and mortality rates: Birmingham, 98, 105–7; Bradford, 138; Bristol, 116–17; Leeds, 61, 67–8, 70, 76; Leicester, 125, 130; Liverpool, 28, 29, 36, 43–4, 47–8
Morpeth, Lord, 134, 164
Mundella, A. J., 148
Municipal authority, 149–73
Municipal corporations, royal commission on, 3, 6–12, 22
Municipal Corporations Act (1835), 11, 13–21 *passim,* 30, 82–3, 91, 112–13, 149, 157–8, 164, 166
Municipal Mortgages Act (1860), 99–100
Municipal socialism, 18, 50, 108, 170–3
Muntz, G. F., 80
Mycock, Alderman T. E., 146

Nettleford, J. S., 170
Newlands, James, 28, 37–8, 43, 100
Nottingham, 2, 4

Oxley, George, 131–2

Index

Parkes, Joseph, 7, 8, 9, 11, 13, 14, 16, 82, 153, 157
Peel, Sir Robert, 4, 6, 10, 13, 14, 15, 88, 89, 90
Picton, J. A., 38
Pigott Smith, James, 98
Place, Francis, 11, 19-21, 153, 154
Playfair, Lyon, 28
Police force, Metropolitan, 3-4, 12, 24-5, 29, 54, 58-9, 88, 89, 113, 115, 132, 141, 142; *Police Act* (1839), 89
Poor Law, the, 29, 80, 131, 132, 139, 147, 152; *Amendment Act* (1834), 152, 160; association for, 28, 47, 112; Board for (1847), 152; commission (1833), 6, 152, 165; *Gilbert's Act*, 80; reform of (1834), 152; report on, 6
Poor Law Union, 18, 152, 154-5
Porcupine, the, 40-1, 42
Prison facilities: Birmingham, 90; Leeds, 58-9, 67
Public Health Act, see under Health and sanitation

Ratepayer associations, 38, 45-6, 75, 82, 97, 99, 126
Rathbone, William, 45-6
Rawlinson, Robert, 93, 94, 128, 136
Redfern, William, 85, 88, 90, 167
Redlich, J., 156, 165, 170
Reform Act: (1832), 5, 13, 84, 113, 115, 123; (1867), 103
Reform Bill, the, 7, 12; riots of 1831, 4, 12
Ripley, H. W., 137
'Rivington Pike' scheme, 33-8, 46

Roberts, Samuel, 139
Robinson, Joseph, 41
Robinson, Dr. M. K., 71
Roebuck, J. A., 19-21, 163-4
Royal Commission on State of Large Towns, 27, 28, 31; *see also* Municipal corporations, Poor Law
Russell, Lord John, 89, 134, 149
Rutter v. Chapman, 55-6, 158
Rylands, Arthur, 99

Salford, 83, 84, 159
Salisbury, Lord, 153
Sanitation, *see* Health and sanitation
Salt, Titus, 132
Scarr, Archie, 75-6, 105
Scholefield, William, 87
Sheffield, 2, 86, 92, 111-48, 166-7; Chartists in, 140, 160; health and sanitation, 111, 140-8; Highways board, 139, 142-6; housing, 140; *Improvement Bill*: (1851), 142; (1858), 144-8; Improvement commission, 139; incorporation of, 111, 139; law enforcement, 140, 142; municipal franchise in, 142; Reform association, 139; Town hall, 144
Sheffield Free Press, The, 141
Shimmin, Hugh, 40-1, 42, 46, 167
Simon, Sir John, 68
Small Tenements Rating Act (1850), 160
Smith, Henry, 95
Society of Merchant Venturers, 112
Stuart Mill, John, 154

Test and Corporation Acts, 4
Times, The, 5, 172
Tinne, John, 37
Toulmin Smith, Joshua, 94, 117, 141, 142–3, 167
Town Clauses Acts, 164–7
Town Crier, the, 40, 103
Trench, Dr. W. S., 43, 47–8

Unincorporated towns, 1, 2, 11, 16, 111, 131
Urban and rural district councils, 155

'Vyrnwy' scheme, the, 46

Walmsley, Joshua, 24–5, 27, 58
'Washburn' scheme, the, 72–3
Water supply, provision of, *see* Health and sanitation
Webb, Beatrice, 18, 120, 149, 164
Webb, Sidney, 18, 120, 149, 164, 171
Whetstone, Joseph, 125–8
White, Sir Thomas, 121
White, William, 108
Will family, the, 118–19
Winks, J. F., 167
Witty, Michael J., 24
Woolcombers Committee, the, 133

York, 111